How To
Hire People
Who Give
A Sh*T

THE GOLDEN RULES

Erika Weinstein

ACKNOWLEDGEMENTS

Thank you to my fabulous husband, Seth, who always has faith in me even when I have doubt.

From the bottom of my heart, thank you Joan Segal and Toni Carrozzo, my colleagues at eTeam Executive Search for your continued support, great advice and bringing humor to the process.

To my clients and candidates, I've learned so much from all of you – thank you!

To my final editor, Savannah Christiansen, who is patient and smart and gets it!

CONTENTS

PREFACE:

Why Do We Work?

Great question. I love starting a hiring conversation with just that: Why do you work? And whom do you want to work with? Yes, I know most of us need to make a living, but we can also be tinkers, tailors, soldiers, spies. What draws someone to a particular path and why? By first examining the "why," perhaps we can approach hiring differently and spark change. Here's the logic: a better hiring process will enable us to make better hiring decisions at every level. We'll save time and money and enjoy our work environment so much more.

As the CEO of eTeam Executive Search, I strive to hire employees and recommend candidates who care, who have *passion* for what they do. Now this might not be a novel concept, but often companies make the mistake of hiring the "safe" candidate, the candidate whose skill set fits the bill, but whose ardor and initiative are lackluster. If we want stars, why don't we shoot for the sky? Why don't we want to hire people who give a sh*t?

I HAPPEN TO GIVE A SH*T,
BUT WHY SHOULD YOU LISTEN TO ME?

Throughout my 20+ year career, I've placed some of the most successful executives at the world's top firms. From tech to media to finance, I maintain an expansive list of clients who know that when they hire me to fill a need, they will not be disappointed. My search techniques are both conventional and, at times, downright maverick, but I don't skip the necessary steps to match the best talent with the right role.

In this book, you'll find my detailed prescription for the best search and hiring practices. But you'll also learn that heart, soul and drive are the keys to success. Whether you're looking to hire or you're looking for your next role, I hope your takeaway from this book will be about people who are passionate. As you journey forward, I'm thrilled to have the opportunity to support you in finding your happiness and passion.

Now let's get started.

INTRODUCTION

Some people call me a headhunter or an executive search consultant--I call myself a passion hunter. I look for the people who give a sh*t, otherwise known as *passionate* people. Those who give a sh*t come in all shapes, sizes and ages. Don't judge a book (or Millennial) by its cover. Passionate people are like diamonds in the rough: You never know where you're going to stumble across one.

When searching for these people, we first need to ask, "What does giving a sh*t mean to you?"

This somewhat basic question often yields complicated answers because to define success for you would be impossible. Only you can determine your happiness and set the goals to achieve your success. My goal in writing this book is to help people hiring or looking for work. It's for people who work at home, in an office, in an auditorium or a rocket ship, even in a space lab in the sky. It's aimed at people who want to make a connection. It's for those who want to optimize their fulfillment.

Without passion, we are adrift in a sea without direction. Before you look to hire the best people, you're going to have to look at your company and define what drives the passion. Doing so will help anchor you and your employees to that kernel of inner passion which keeps you working. When the time comes to bring new people onto your team, keep in mind that you're not just hiring a body with a skill set. Put the résumé aside and start interviewing with the intent of getting to know the person sitting in front of you. Don't get caught up with the factoids of their background--yet. Before anything else, you first need to understand your and their passions. Only then can you speak to cultural fit.

At the beginning of my recruiting career, I made the typical rookie mistake of relying solely on the résumé to determine if a candidate was a good fit for my client.

Over twenty years ago, on day one in fact, I fell into my first recruiting assignment. I was working for a company called Howard Sloan Professional Services and I was brand new to recruiting, with no one to teach me the ropes. Sitting at my desk, calling my contacts, the phone rings. Debra who was my client from my previous career, called and ask if I would fill some positions for her promotional agency based in Dallas.

I couldn't control myself and I blurted out: "Holy sh*t, Debra today's my first day. I have no experience as a recruiter! Are you sure that you want to work with me?" "You know our culture, people and goals better than any recruiter we've worked with." I was a recruiter for all of 4 hours, working in New York City, and I didn't know the talent pool in Dallas, but I remember what Debra said, "you'll figure it out."

Debra's words didn't sink in with me right away. Little did I know at the time that I already had the innate skills of recruiting, but in terms how to put my skills to work, I was clueless. So I went for the next best strategy: I leaned on who and what I already knew. Armed with the Red Book (think LinkedIn of the pre-internet age) that Debra sent me and with my knowledge of the agency, I started to, as sales people like to call it, "dial for dollars." I was nervous. There were so many unknowns and I didn't have the answers. I took a deep breath, picked up the phone and called an executive I knew. "Tim, hi. It's Erika. Weinstein. Do you have a moment? I could really use your advice on a position I'm working on." I didn't bullshit him by faking that I knew what I was talking about. I needed his advice. I was interested in hearing what he thought. Tim was amazing. He gave me his time, expertise and he gave me names and contact information to some of the best talent in the Dallas market.

I recruited a candidate, John, who fit all of the requirements on Debra's list for the perfect employee. I faxed her immediately with his résumé (that was our speedy form of communication back then).

"Oh, we already know John" she told me.

That was my first mistake. I should have asked if both my client and candidate if they knew each other.

Debra is the kind of person who would never say a bad word about anybody, so I had to probe her on why John wasn't a good fit. I quickly figured out that she didn't like that John was a lone player.

While I had been so focused on looking at people's skills, I missed out on searching for those people who would fit in with Debra's company culture - COLLABORATIVE.

My learning curve was fast and steep. I made a lot of mistakes back then, but through trial and error, recruiting became something like a sport, kind of like golfing or tennis. I realized that it's not about each stroke, but it's consistency, practice, failure and success that really makes us great at what we do. Bottom line, if you don't have passion then you'll never be successful.

I jumped into recruiting with two feet, fortified with authenticity and integrity. I didn't call candidates with the perfect position; I didn't have all the answers, but I was real and was interested in my candidates' and clients' success and happiness.

Additionally, I learned an important lesson. Treat everyone with respect, because you never know who they know and what position might be right for them in the future. This philosophy is especially profound in today's social media society, when candidates can walk out of an interview and start texting/posting about you and your company. Their interview experience can go viral even before the elevator gets to the lobby. A bad reputation affects your employees' mojo, not to mention, making finding someone infinitely more difficult. I can't count how many times I've started a search, calling the bulls-eye candidates only to learn that they've been turned off by the process, the recruiter disseminating false information, the interviewer shows up late or sometimes not at all, the position has been open too long or there's unrealistic expectations. A poorly planned and executed talent search process is passion's kiss of death. Finding the right position/candidate is about the journey, but if you turn off candidates, they won't spread the word to the potential candidates who are two degrees removed from your network.

In the following chapters, my guide to hiring the passionate people will help fuel your company's success. Before we begin, you must first learn to identify passion, what's important to you and what does your company care about. Only then can we look outward to hiring the right people who give a sh*t.

"I know I said I wanted you to give a sh*t, but not literally."

CHAPTER ONE:

GIVING A SH*T

WHAT IS PASSION?

Some people are born with a passion. They know what they want to do from birth. Some, for instance, are born with a musical or mathematical aptitude (I'm not one of those people). My daughter has always been fascinated by the human body. I remember picking her up from a kindergarten interview and found her holding a hypodermic needle from one of those toy doctor kits. She looked up at the teacher, with her big eyes and a look of innocence and said, "I'm going to put a hole in your arm and I'm not going to get you a Band-Aid. You know how when the blood goes through your body it will come out through this hole and you're going to die." I was mortified. I turned to the teacher and half-jokingly said, "Would you believe me if I said she was going to be a future Stephen King novelist?" The teacher didn't laugh.

I took my daughter to see a therapist the next day, who assured me that a five year old talking about death was completely normal. What was not apparent was "how did she know about the circulatory system". Long story short, she took out a book about the human body from the library - she was "hooked". Now, years later, my daughter is studying to be a doctor. Clearly, her passion for medicine had became apparent in early childhood.

For most of us, however, we need a bit more time to figure out our passion path, what kind of career "fits" our innate strengths and personality. Don't get discouraged, like anything, trial and error are part of the journey to success. Often, during our journey, we find something we are good at and our passion builds as we develop.

Passionate people don't care what they look like or how much money they have in the bank. Passionate people set a goal, perhaps one that might seem slightly out of reach, and practice until the goal is achieved. Passion isn't about skill sets or brains. It's about winning: attaining the ultimate prize, but the prize is different for everyone.

When I think of someone full of passion, John Young, a triathlete and the first person with dwarfism to finish a full-distance Ironman competition comes to mind. Despite people telling him throughout his life that he was too short and too small to ever compete in races like the Ironman, John saw his situation merely from a different starting point. "I don't think my race is any harder, it's just my race" he told CNN.[1] What's more, he noted that, "with shorter arms and legs, it takes more strokes to swim or steps to run the same distance as an average-sized triathlete. I have done the calculations and determined with my 20-inch wheels, I need to pedal at least 35 percent more revolutions in order to go the same distance as someone using

1 *Athlete Won't Let Dwarfism Stop Ironman Dream: John Young Is Hoping to Become the First Person with Dwarfism to Complete an Ironman Triathlon.* CNN, n.d. https://www.cnn.com/videos/health/2016/11/18/fit-nation-ironman-john-young-dwarfism.cnn/video/playlists/fit-nation/.

a 27-inch wheel." His criteria for success were different from every-one else and he succeeded because he's passionate and he sticks to a plan that is tailored to his own needs and wishes.

WHY DOES PASSION MATTER?

Passion is the elixir of success. It's what makes us want to expand our performance to the max. How do we get this elixir? Well, neuroscience has the chemical recipe with the main ingredients: Dopamine, Oxytocin, Serotonin and Endorphin. According to Dr. Loretta Graziano Breuning, when we come to work, we come with a built-in chemistry that gives us the ability to protect, trust, fight and or flee.

Dopamine: energizes you when you find a new way to meet a need. It's the brain's signal that a reward is at hand.

Serotonin: rewards you with a good feeling when you gain a social advantage. We make careful decisions about when to assert and when to defer. Serotonin is released when we see ourselves in the one-up position.

Oxytocin: is the good feeling of social trust. We can relax and lower our guard in the presence of trusted others. Touch and trust go together because those close enough to touch you are close enough to hurt you.

Endorphin: masks pain with euphoria. This allows us to protect our-selves. Endorphin kicks in for emergencies, i.e., "Runner's high" only happens if you run to the point of pain. [2]

2 Loretta Graziano Breuning. *Habits of a Happy Brain: Retrain Your Brain to Boost Your Serotonin, Dopamine, Oxytocin, & Endorphin Levels.* F + W Media, 2015.

Harnessing and understanding this chemistry is key to creating balance at work. We know, for instance, that a person's motivation is born from a combination of a natural propensity to be good at something, combined with a reward system that nurtures excellence and passion. Human beings need to feel purposeful, recognized, and wanted. That's why when we perform consistently and produce worthy results, we expect to be rewarded, recognized and praised. Often when people perfect their craft and hone their skills, passion grows. When passion is the driver, success often follows. So how do we cultivate passion in the workplace? There are a few basic ingredients we must consider: leadership + peers + environment + monetary rewards. If you add these ingredients together, combined with how tolerant a company is of taking risks + sharing + f*cking up + listening, you usually get something that looks like the company culture. Having a first-hand relationship with your culture is imperative to hiring people who give a sh*t, because your culture has to match candidates' passions.

THE KEYS TO PASSION

LEADERSHIP

Leaders who really get to know their people are more likely to elicit passion. If you want your employees to perform at their maximum capacity, you need to establish personal relationships. Eat lunch in the lunch room instead of the board room. Ask people about their hobbies and dreams. Even a quick, "how was your weekend?" or "how's your family?" can pick up team morale. When we establish personal connections, we are more likely to develop a cohesive workforce. When people's hearts are into their work, there is a beating heart in your company.

In *Leaders Eat Last*, author and motivational speaker, Simon Sinek, proposes a concept of leadership that has little to do with authority, management acumen or even being in charge. True leadership, Sinek says, is about empowering others to achieve things they didn't think possible. Exceptional organizations, he says, "prioritize the well-being of their people and, in return, their people give everything they've got to protect and advance the well-being of one another and the organization."

Whether we're leading armies, multinational corporations or a fledgling home-based business, Sinek's message is the same. "We all have the responsibility to become the leaders we wish we had."[3] Without strong, personable leadership, passion can never emerge in the workplace.

PEERS

Leaders who cultivate relationships amongst peers tend to create positive cultures driven by collaboration and self-pride. Don't worry about individual performers; the rock stars on your team will push the envelope for others and the team will subsequently feed off of that energy. People truly become co-workers when they start to feel part of the team. They may even become more than just workaday colleagues. I've met some of my dearest friends on the job. Chalk it up to "The Law of Connectivity." Simply put, we tend to like people who are like us. Maybe it's because we crave empathy, and who's apt to empathize with us if not someone who shares our interests and goals? When we meaningfully connect with our peers, we feel happy and we excel.

---

3 Sinek, Simon. *Leaders Eat Last: Why Some Teams Pull Together and Others Don't.* Penguin, 2014.

ENVIRONMENT

Great, caring leadership combined with peer-to-peer collaboration often fosters creativity and ingenuity. When our peers are passionate and excited about the same things as we are, this generally creates a positive and uplifting environment. However, there are CEOs who don't value culture and prescribe to the old-fashioned idea that money is the only reward. Today I would argue that the companies we admire most are innovative and often are recognized as the best places to work. For many of us, it isn't easy to maintain a positive attitude at work, especially during economic downturns or unforeseen market factors. Achieving a culturally positive environment at times seems insurmountable. As anyone who's been working for a few years knows, there are going to be ups and downs, and it's the optimistic people and companies who always seem to come out on top. It takes work, imagination and planning to create a passionate environment.

Regardless whether you're a fan of Facebook, the company continually tops the charts as one of the best places to work, partly due to its company perks and supportive work environment. Ranking No.1 on Glassdoor's Annual Employee Choice Awards, Facebook employees report feeling valued and trusted.[4] They're also given a fair amount of autonomy, allowing employees to build strong relationships with people of all ranks. According to one program manager, Facebook is genuine when it says it wants to build a more connected world, inside and outside of the company's walls. "The openness is a real thing, we're trusted to do the right thing, mistakes are expected, being yourself is important and encouraged…the mission of making

---

4 Glassdoor. "Glassdoor's 2018 Best Places to Work: Employee Choice Awards." https://www.glassdoor.com/Award/Best-Places-to-Work-LST_KQ0,19.htm.

the world a more open and connected place isn't just a cool phrase because it guides everything. It's not about us, it's about everyone else" they write Glassdoor. Facebook, by encouraging a collaborative environment (and preserving the original, scrappy, startup culture vibe) infuses the workplace with positivity, helping to fuel its success.[5]

MONETARY REWARDS

Yet, there's no dismissing the power of money as a motivator. Most people are inspired to perform if there's something "in it" for them. Monetary gain is not always the most important criterion for happiness, but getting compensated for a job well done can go a long way in spurring employee initiative. At times compensation plans, such as commissions and bonus plans, help to build team morale. At the same time compensation should never be left up to interpretation. Establishing a plan in which monetary rewards are laid out from the get-go is extremely important in setting goals and expectations. That way, there's no confusion over the reward, plus it keeps things moving efficiently.

---

5 See: McCracken, Harry. "How Facebook Keeps Scaling Its Culture." *Fast Company*, November 24, 2015. https://www.fastcompany.com/3053776/how-facebook-keeps-scaling-its-culture.

"I said that I have golden handcuffs, these aren't necessary."

STEWART'S GOLDEN HANDCUFFS

Loving your job while striving for monetary rewards is a complicated relationship. Early on in my career, I recruited a gentleman named Stewart, who was working at Goldman Sachs at the time. I called Stewart and went through my usual spiel: "Hi, how are you? I'm wondering if you could help me. I'm working on a project and I was told that you are the financial marketing guru I need to talk to."

Stewart, before letting me even finish, let me know that he was "happy." I asked him what would make him even happier. Stewart thought about it and said, "working on the consumer side of financial marketing." At the time, the field of consumer financial marketing was just burgeoning, kickstarting the idea that day traders could take ownership of their deals on Wall St. It seemed promising to me that he was interested in this emerging field, so I continued to ask him about it.

"But I have golden handcuffs and you're never going to be able to afford me" Stewart said to me. With that, he hung up the phone. At the time, I was still a little new to the game and didn't know what he was talking about. Golden handcuffs?

I called my all-knowing brother who worked on the trading floor and asked, "Joe, what are golden handcuffs?" He explained that its the bonus at the end of the year which makes up a good portion of income, and consequently, how your employer has "handcuffed" you to your seat. I thought about it and called Stewart the next day, starting with, "Stewart, let's talk about jewelry.(golden handcuffs)" He laughed.

When we got to talking, I learned that he was truly passionate about pursuing something on the consumer side of his job. I recommended that we put the subject of money on the back burner, since my client would pay for the right person, and ultimately I convinced him to take the interview. Stewart ended up working at the position for nearly two decades and was quite happy. What his happiness came down to was a question of putting aside the money and getting to his passion.

TAKING RISKS

Without the ability to go where no man has gone before (I'm a Trekkie), there is no discovery or innovation. The unknown and untested is always risky. To quote Captain Kirk, "the greatest danger facing us is ourselves, and irrational fear of the unknown. There is no such thing as the unknown. Only things temporarily hidden, temporarily not understood." A company's tolerance of risk reveals a thing or two about how open they are to discovery and innovation.

For the most part, if you research a variety of companies, it will quickly become apparent that they consist of different people and personalities. There's usually the CEO, the entrepreneur, the founders, the bookkeepers, the researchers and the analysts. To say these workers differ in their boiling point for risk is putting it mildly. I often like to think of them as members of a family road trip. The driver is the CEO, who decides which car we drive, and which road to take. As the CEO, I'm often the decision-maker on our destination, but there are so many decisions to make before we even get in the car. Where are we going to eat? What will we see along the way? The success of the road trip relies on planning and having the right people with us. So too the success of the business road trip. There may be wrong turns and bad roads ahead, but detailed research, planning and hiring the best people who share our passion and vision can help circumvent some of the unnecessary risk while ensuring that the necessary risk (mid-trip stop at the world's largest donut) is pursued and enjoyed, when appropriate.

SHARING

Sharing information, our viewpoints and experiences, especially in the information age, is imperative for a team to function effectively. We are constantly bombarded with new information and in order to make sure colleagues are well-informed, companies must create a communication style that works for everyone. My business in particular relies on sharing professional opinions and expertise. We call on close-knit experts in our industries for referrals and references on potential candidates.

Sharing with your team promotes growth. Young people come to work for you because they want to learn, grow and participate. They look to your leadership for your knowledge and experiences and they want to spread their wings and test their new skills. Without a sharing culture, you create silos where knowledge can become entrapped. If you can't share, you can't teach. The CEO who can't teach their team is a CEO who will not grow their company. It's impossible to have a one-man band in this day and age.

F*CKING UP--EVERYONE IS DOING IT!

We often talk about onboarding, giving the company newbie a manual to learn protocol and procedures. Companies might have training seminars, webcasts or onboarding meetings to acclimate their new hires. Onboarding *per se* isn't a problem, but all too often there's a mismatch between the approach and the desired results. Rather than dictating how to behave under all circumstances, companies would fare better if their onboarding practices promoted curiosity. When people are inspired to think creatively, they might fail, but they may also succeed above and beyond their wildest dreams. For the most part, onboarding practices don't elicit a trial and error mentality or even the likes of, "let me show you, now you go out and adapt and make it your own." The first message we often give our employees is: "Do it the right way," or "This is the way we do it here." For some people this might be just the right approach and environment. There are high achievers who like to be told how things are done. Then there are the great thinkers, doers and originals who like to test boundaries. Think Steve Jobs or Bill Gates. They need freedom to f*ck up.

Whether you're recruiting or being recruited, you need to take this facet of work culture into consideration. If you're a curious worker and someone who enjoys taking risks, but the hiring manager likes things to be done by the book, even if you're the world's most qualified person for the position, don't take the job. You won't be happy at the company. They've been doing the same thing for a gazillion years and they're unlikely to suddenly change stripes for you.

Most people don't even think about the freedom to f*ck up as part of a candidate's or company's personality before they make a hiring match. We are so caught up in concrete skills and concrete explanations that we forget to examine what is at the core of our behavior and our impulses. To err is to be human. Today, though, with the world at our fingertips, society doesn't make room for mistakes. Both at work and at play, the expectation is that our answers should be perfect, and when we don't know, we ask Siri. We are more interested in the answer than in the journey of exploration.

Hiring is not just about the goal, but also about the journey. Take a professional baseball player who is just starting out. They might not throw the ball straight the first hundred or so times. But with practice, the player eventually connects and, well, the rest is history: a baseball star is born. Remember the journey when you hire. It's important to the team.

THE PHILOSOPHY OF "NEXT"

Obviously, we can't expect that people's' f*ck ups are not going to have any negative consequences. The trick is in finding the balance between providing space and freedom to screw up and making catastrophic mistakes that cost money, jobs and sometimes put us out of business. I found that one of the most freeing feelings is allowing my employees to make mistakes.

Before my aha moment, my staff was constantly running into my office with every little task. It's only normal for people to be afraid of the phone, and most of my employees were nervous about cold-calling candidates when they first started. They worried they wouldn't sound good and that they only had one shot at reaching someone. I had to constantly remind them that (1) being human was not perfect and mistakes, bad calls happen - NEXT! Sometimes you just need to say "next" and move on. My micro-managing style was causing me to be an ineffective business owner and a lousy leader. I became aware that often the recruiter knew the answer, but their fear of failure was getting in their way of "doing it" themselves. Truly great leaders create a culture that allows for risk. Otherwise the leader is too busy being everyone else's assistant.

To rectify this fear-driven culture, I instituted "the f*ck up policy," which meant that when you make a mistake, you had to write it down, learn from it, don't do it again and feel free to make the next mistake. However, if you make the same mistake repeatedly, then you need to own your behavior and it's time for us to talk about the mistake. I also instituted the "next" philosophy. You can't change a mistake made in the past, so get over it––now. If you learn from your mistake, it's onto the next one.

Of course I also put guardrails in place so that mistakes become lessons and not catastrophic, non-recoverable deeds. Establishing golden rules for your workers is a good way to provide structure without being too strict. Some of my golden rules include: don't send your client a résumé without consent; don't tell the candidates what the position pays; ask if it's a good time to talk, etc. My executives or financial officer must okay all contracts, but I continually find areas where I feel comfortable giving people the freedom to explore. If that means making a mistake, I have to understand that no mistake is the end of the world.

MY PERSONAL F*CK UP

Early in my career, I left my position at the advertising firm Saatchi and Saatchi to start my own company called Corporate Concierge. It originated from an idea: "Our clients live such busy lives, we want to do nice things for them—you know, book dinner reservations, send a baby gift, get tickets to the Raiders game." Back in the day, you needed people to physically execute these tasks. That's where Corporate Concierge came in. The concept was a little ahead of its time; there was no internet, so it was technically difficult to do nice things for others with the speed of TaskRabbit.

Without the internet, I had to rely on phone books (ancient data-base). I busted my butt cold-calling companies as I fought vigorously to develop my client list, but ultimately, we were understaffed and out of time. With just an idea and no internet to keep things moving smoothly, Corporate Concierge simply could not deliver the ritzy services that could lure corporations on board. I had to be realistic, so I made the decision to "fold'em knew when to hold'em" closed the company and moved on.

For me, every day can be a hardship. I can't spell for sh*t. I dial phone numbers wrong and I management style is referred to by employees as helter-skelter. My team must follow the bouncing ball––typical style for an entrepreneur. What I do well, however, is inspire, infuse passion and encourage my team to F*CK UP. I want them to own their responsibilities and decisions, good and bad. It's the only way people can grow. Without the ability to f*ck-up, we become stymied and safe. Safe is good for driving on the highway, but not always for building a business.

GOLDEN RULE: Experimenting is the key to innovation

I've realized during my entrepreneurial career that I've probably f*ck up more than most people. I make more sales calls and get more rejections than acceptances. I've started businesses that failed, like Corporate Concierge, because I didn't have the right network or technology and didn't do enough homework before I opened my doors. I've said the wrong things during meetings (like telling an off-color joke to the president of a major cosmetics company––I didn't get the business!). I've also had excellent adventures, made and lost a ton of money and met people from all walks of life. It's hard to earn a reward if you're too afraid to take risks! The trick is to ask questions and listen.

LISTENING IS MORE IMPORTANT THAN TALKING, TEXTING, EVEN EMAILING

LEAD WITH LISTENING

The most interesting business leaders I've met understand the importance of developing their listening skills. Listening is key in creating real, working relationships between employees and management and creating winning teams. Listening gives you the advantage of learning information, whether from an employee, a client or a colleague. When you have the floor, you are usually presenting, dictating, directing, teaching and or sharing, but often the talker/presenter is not getting verbal information.

I believe that our ability to create and produce correlates from how well we're able to process information. Well-developed listening skills positively impact our business and personal interactions and depending on the situation, may determine whether customers and even colleagues' husbands, wives or partners stay or go.

I have certainly lost potential business because I simply wasn't listening. I had my own agenda and wanted their needs to fit my goals. Listening is hard to master and we constantly have to remind ourselves to actively engage in conversation by remaining present. Which is why the number one tool I have in business is asking questions and listening for the answers.

During the hiring process, asking the right questions and observing people's responses is imperative. For example, if a candidate mentions that he did not "feel appreciated" in his last role, it's important not to let this statement go overlooked. Feeling appreciated and needed, as we covered earlier, is one of the most important factors in enjoying a position. If the candidate did not feel appreciated because he did not receive a raise, that is very different from the morale zapper of not getting recognition for a project that was well received.

> **GOLDEN RULE:** When you are actively
> listening, it's really hard to f*ck up.

QUESTIONS TO GAUGE CULTURE

There are many details, nuances, sounds and sights that make up culture. Before I even start a search, I make sure to get a firm feel on what my client does and what their company culture is like.

Here are a few bullets I like to tick off when working with a new client:

- What values drive your company?

- What are you personally passionate about?

- Describe your favorite employee.

- What's the company vibe? (Young, hip, quiet, noisy, athletes, artists?)

- What does the office look like? (Funky, conservative?)

- Why should someone work for you?

- Why do you need to hire this person?

- What are they supposed to accomplish?

- In one word, describe the most important attribute a person should have.

- How do you know your goals are realistic?

- Is there anyone on your team you may have consider for this position?

Hiring is a team sport, I make it my mission to interview several different people from all departments of the company to get the full picture.

The first question I ask the CEO on down to the executive assistant:

"WHY DO YOU WORK HERE?"

People will often say the company "does great work and has great clients." Classic response that says little to nothing. I'll follow up with, "I understand your competitor delivers great work and wins top accounts too. Why not work for them?" We need to find the specifics of what sets you and your company apart from the competitors. What's the special sauce, that help pinpoint candidates that will be a good match? Often, the answer includes feeling valued and that you make a difference at the company.

EMOTIONS AND YOUR ENVIRONMENT

Often, people will report feeling afraid or anxious at work. In many workplaces the tone come from the top. Leaders are responsible for setting company culture; behaviors coming from the top permeate within the entire environment. Anxiety, fear and excitement often feel the same to us. While anxiety and fear are debilitating and counterproductive, excitement, though sometimes misunderstood as anxiety or fear, really is a catalyst for healthy competition. My comedy coach, yes, I do standup, constantly says, "don't think afraid, get yourself into the zone by stating, 'I'm excited to get up there, it's going to be fun'". Turning our fears into excitement is energizing and motivating.

A couple of years ago I walked into Tech Company where the noise level was off the charts. No one had an office, even the CEO sat in the middle of a bullpen. When people had a meeting or needed privacy, there were glass rooms at all four corners of the floor. For me it was a madhouse, to my clients it was exciting. What works for one person doesn't necessarily work for the next. To understand a company's culture, leadership and environment, put yourself in their shoes and go exploring.

DARIN'S REWARD

Darin is a chief creative officer for a leading global experiential agency, and he once called me to help hire a digital creative lead. The first thing I noticed when entering his office is the bean bag chairs, Lego tables and white boards covered in graffiti. Contrary to the décor, there were very few people in plain sight and the place was super quiet.

First question, "Where's your team?" The funny thing is, I remember Darin looking around, equally puzzled, but his quick answer was that they were on a pitch. Next question: "If everyone in the company was here, what would I see, feel and experience?" And finally, I asked, "What does passion look like for you?"

He proceeded to show me the creativity involved in broadcasting a sporting event for a major telecom company and the ideas that went into it. Great program, but so what? I pressed Darin for his gut feelings: "Why do you work here? Why do you create? How does creating make you feel, and does your management recognize your value and appreciate your talents and contributions? How do you feel when you walk into work every morning?"

Darin has a proven track record of creating award-winning programs. But he had a hard time expressing the passion of his agency and why he works there. In digging deeper, I learned that he is driven by two things: praise from the client, who constantly come back for more providing Darin what he desires - personal gratification.

Let's start with praise. Darin's events create buzz and drive results, and his management recognizes his value. In his three years at the agency, he has consistently won internal rewards, raises and increased responsibilities and the opportunity to build a team. We tend to remember our good days over our bad days and for Darin, the good days outnumbered the bad. It comes down to a few basics: feeling good and getting rewarded.

CHAPTER TWO:

PASSION, IN ALL ITS STYLES AND FORMS

DIVERSITY OF PASSION

If I had a dollar for every leader I've interviewed who is unaware of, or unable to articulate, what is the uniqueness of their company, I'd be a gazillionaire. However, when I ask them about what they are passionate about in their personal lives, most people are excited and can elaborate with real emotions. In today's world of blurring the time we spend in the office and working outside the office, shouldn't we be equally in touch with our work passions? And if we don't have this awareness, how can we effectively recruit a team that is expected to be passionate and drive results?

Your definition of passion is singular, but you may want to consider a couple of ingredients to keep in mind when building your company.

PASSION ON FIRE

Stuart is the CMO for a high-end luxury brand and he essentially lives on a plane. He's a can-do person, constantly traveling and on-call always jetting off somewhere to promote his brand. I usually only speak to him between flights at the airport, which makes him difficult to pin down and meet with potential candidates. I once asked him, "do you ever take time off?" He told me no. He should, but he doesn't. Stuart loves what he does. He lives and breathes his brand and enjoys the perks associated with his company - working with high net-worth clients, expensive dinners, fundraisers and exotic travel. Stuart's lifestyle isn't for everyone, but his work/life is a 24/7 blur between work and home. His ability to work anywhere or anytime creates a seamless lifestyle that is fueled by his passions.

Of course the passion flame can fluctuate between pilot light or raging fire mode. At other times, it's just a steady simmer and things cook away on all four burners. Passion originates from within and each person is responsible for bringing that passion to the office, whether the office is at home or on an airplane or in an office.

I work with a woman named Toni. Toni is a uber organized kind of person who loves getting everything into the right order. Toni tells me that she goes home at night and thinks about how to put our information into our database, constantly looking for better ways to make sure we maintain our integrity and up-to-date freshness of our intellectual property. I haven't asked her to do this. I've never asked her to work evenings or weekends, but for Toni, plugging in data relaxes her. She loves order from the inside out, bringing the passion with her from home to the office and back again. When she interacts with clients, her passion shines through and she's constantly receiving positive feedback from her clients and candidates. Toni's passion allows her to occupy a specific niche within our company where her fire can always stay lit.

COMPARTMENTALIZED FIRE

The database lit Toni's fire, correct? Well, not exactly. The passion's been lit because of her interactions not only with her co-workers and her hiring manager, but also with her clients and her candidates. It's how they make her feel; it's her sense of accomplishment that she can bring home at the end of the day and continue working. Her passion bleeds over into more than one aspect of her life.

Others are more inclined to a lifestyle almost completely opposite of Toni's compartmentalization mindset. While I was writing this book, my editor asked me if people who compartmentalize their emotions and thinking can be passionate. Great question. There are people who function best by sitting down to work totally charged and by leaving it behind when they go home. Conversely, we don't want people coming to work who bring their home baggage with them into the office. I believe it's important to be flexible. Not everyone thinks about work 24/7. In other words, the Stephen Stills' *Love the One You're With* ethos is not for everyone, but works for others. I've met some bosses who expect their employees to be accessible 24/7 so for them, the folks who naturally compartmentalize may not be the best fit. Personally, I love these people. They live in the moment and tend to laser-focus on the task in front of them.

Take 'mediapreneur' Samantha, for instance. She's your typical high-powered digital media executive who pulls in about $850,000 per year. Samantha's husband is a successful doctor who works long hours; they have three kids and are contemplating getting a puppy *(she must be crazy)*. I've never socialized with Samantha. I've only experienced her in a business setting, where she is quick, kind and focused. She asks probing questions, listens to her co-workers and is totally engaged in the process of decision-making. When I asked Samantha how she balances all the intricate parts of her life, her answer surprised me: "Well, it's my clothes. When I put on my work clothes, I play the part of executive. When I get to go home and put on my sweatpants, I play the mom part. " Of course, I find this to be pretty funny, but she goes on to say that clothes help her visualize the role she has at work, at home and when she's out on the town with her husband and friends. Her clothes symbolize the diversity of her life, the energy she brings to the people around her and the simple fact that she doesn't have to be just one person. Changing her outfit allows her to seamlessly transition between roles. This fashionista is mommy, president, honey and at parent-teacher conferences, Mrs. Wonderful. Sometimes it's easier to separate work from play when we're suited up for the task at hand.

"I know this isn't where you live, but I really believe in going the extra mile."

PASSION CAN GO AWRY

Passion is absolutely essential, but it can also veer off course. When this happens, it's like an explosion going off. It looks like anarchy. It looks like yelling and screaming—whether you're at home and it's directed towards your kids or you're at work and your temper flares every time someone puts you on hold. I've known hiring managers and CEOs of companies who think that they are helping people by yelling at them and demeaning them in order to yield better results. I personally don't believe this is a productive form of management: this is passion gone awry. Rage is not productive and usually, it does not work as a motivator. If a company has a yeller, and I discover the lead candidate is easily excitable, I usually 'pull' the candidate off the list. The goal in hiring is solving a problem and finding people is to find positions for people where both the individual and the company will be happy with the placement long-term.

Passion can sometimes blur our ability to make good decisions, especially when we react to a situation and forget to weigh all of our options. When we are on sensory overload, we tend to make snap decisions when really, we should try to pause and reflect on the situation. Passion can also make people feel superfluous, such as in the case of Craig, the CEO of an advertising agency. Craig was so obsessed with his company's bottom line, took too much on himself, and didn't trust his team to do their jobs efficiently. His employees never gave him a reason to feel this way, but Craig could only see one path to reach his desired result. His passion for perfection, at times, bubbled into anger, leading him to shriek and even throw things at his employees. Needless to say, this type of hostile behavior is not sustainable and doesn't lead to corporate growth. I found out the hard way that Craig's passion for his business was poisonous and the people we recruited for his team never lasted long. I finally had to "fire the client" because I didn't have the heart to place people in such a volatile environment.

Great leaders tend to achieve greatness with the help of others, but what about our lone wolves? There are people who are blessed with specific skill sets but can't necessarily work well with a team. Their managers may opt to let them work on projects only by themselves. Many brilliant people are like this, and sometimes it can be beneficial. In my own experience, lone wolves never prosper for long without the help of others. The trick is to help this person merge with the pack sooner rather than later, before their passion spirals past the point of productivity. In an article for *Entrepreneur*, author Chris Penttila offers up a few strategies for achieving this integration. Penttila quotes leaders who say the best method is to "figure out their strengths, and find someone in the company who can connect on some level with this non-people person, at least enough to keep projects moving."[6] Others say the most effective strategy is to provide structure for the lone wolves, while making sure they still feel their freedom, meaning you shouldn't hesitate to hand them entire projects, but make sure they actually do want to work alone or not. It may take a few tries, but working with these lone wolves closely before passion spirals is key to harnessing their capabilities.

ANDREW--WHAT DOES PASSION LOOK LIKE?

When you step into a new relationship with a client, keep in mind that everyone comes to the table with their own likes, dislikes, and prejudices. Though it's technically illegal, ageism, racism and sexism

6 Penttila, Chris. "Managing the 'Lone Wolf.'" *Entrepreneur*, April 1, 2005. https://www.entrepreneur.com/article/76968.

rage on in the workplace. It can be tricky to navigate those prejudices, especially when they blind the client from seeing the brilliance
of a potential candidate and impede on their own success.

Years ago, I had a client who was looking to hire a head of marketing for their startup technology company, and the owners (two
guys named Dan, both very cool) shocked me when they flat out
said, "Erika, one of the things we have to have is a good-looking person." I took pause at that, and actually I was offended. I said, "Really?
You only do business with good-looking people?" "Yeah, we only
do business with good-looking people, that's our rule. If you were a
dog, we wouldn't do business with you." Geez, these guys had some
serious prejudices.

I found out that the "Dans" were only half-kidding. What the Dans
meant by "good looking" was that there had to be a spark of genius,
a spark that could make them money, meaning, I better find a brilliant candidate for the role at this company. This is before LinkedIn,
Facebook and all other forms of social media existed. I wound up
recruiting somebody who was recommended to me, a guy named
Andrew Lona, who was working somewhere in Asia. There was no
video chatting, so I had to have several phone conversations with
him in order to get the 'full picture.' Andrew was ridiculously smart,
had a great voice and was pumped about data storage. He taught
me more about that industry than I ever could have imagined. Who
knew data storage could be so sexy?

Andrew emerged, to me, as the passionate candidate the Dans were
looking for, but when I met Andrew, he wasn't exactly a beauty
queen. All I could think of was, "Oh my God, they only want to
interview somebody good-looking!" Yet every time Andrew opened

his mouth, he was so f*cking beautiful. I absolutely saw him in the role. He was also clearly a wonderful human being, which was more than I could say at that point about the supposedly looks-obsessed Dans. I had them interview several people. I made sure that everybody was passionate and somewhat attractive and educated. Now I was presenting Andrew, with that fire that you just want to hire.

I did Andrew's writeup, emphasizing how he was super funny and smart, and that he knew the industry. I called up the Dans and I said, "I found this candidate…" The Dans were impressed by my description and agreed to an interview.

The moral of the story is that Andrew Lona was one of their best hires. As their CMO, he helped position the company for an acquisition by HP. Andrew, the Dans and the whole rest of the company made a wad of money. I learned the two Dan's were into passion, making it happen and having fun while making money. If I could help them see around their surface obsession with looks, then I've done my job. Good-looking indeed.

PASSION SURVEY

The following is a list of questions to keep in mind when you set out to define the passion which drives you and your company:

1. **What puts a smile on your face?**

   Take a moment and think about something that makes you happy. It doesn't have to be awe inspiring, just something that brings you joy.

2. **What comes naturally to you?**

    We all tend to do things that we love because usually, we are good at what we love.

3. **Who inspires you?**

    We often admire ordinary people for doing extraordinary things. Their deeds and accomplishments spark admiration.

4. **What would you do if you knew you could not fail?**

    How would you live, what would you do and whom would you choose to spend your time with? It's scary to work outside of your comfort zone, but sometimes experiencing something different can be very inspiring.

5. **What do you love to share?**

    For some people, it's family, ideas or a meal. If you have trouble identifying something you are passionate about, take a look at what you're sharing.

6. **What really happens when you fail?**

    Most of us can't deal with failure and making mistakes. Instead of focusing on the bad, what would happen if instead you used your stumbling and soldiering on as a way to learn lessons and improve in your field?

7. **What's your bucket list?**

    Don't wait until the end. It's usually too late.
    Why not do it now?

"Jeff you don't think you're taking
this business is a tribe shtick
too seriously?"

CHAPTER THREE:

FINDING CULTURE

DEVELOP AND DEFINE YOUR CULTURE

> **GOLDEN RULE:** Culture is not just having the core values of your company painted on the wall.

To understand a thriving company culture, I called up Sarah, Director of Human Resources at Blue Chip Marketing Worldwide, where the work environment is innovative, and employees report that they can maintain a work/life balance while also adhering to the "play hard, work harder" mentality.[7] I knew Sarah was a wiz at maintaining happy and engaged employees so I inquired about her company's "special sauce." Sarah laughed and said, "I knew you were going to ask me this question." She conceded that articulating culture, values and vision isn't easy, but after I dug a bit, she started opening up about the way corporate values impact more than just performance:

---

7 "Blue Chip Marketing Worldwide Reviews." Glassdoor. Accessed December 5, 2018. https://www.glassdoor.com/Reviews/Blue-Chip-Marketing-Worldwide-Reviews-E403219.htm.

"In order to be genuine in your job, your culture needs to go beyond the office community—it speaks to the larger community in which we live." At Blue Chip, there are programs designed to promote such core values as: "Being true, compassionate, kind, collaborative" and "having pride in ownership and accountability." Sarah and her team have developed organizational activities to get people engaged. "We have a program called BeCause (BC for Blue Chip), where everyone gets one day off to go out into the community and give back." As a result the employees come back energized, which says a lot about the company. Blue Chip is not just about the bottom line and revenue. They also recognize that there's a bigger world out there and that we all have to live in it. Creating a winning culture is not something that happens inside of the office; it's something that personifies your team and their lives beyond work life.

QUESTIONS TO ASK A PROSPECTIVE CANDIDATE THAT TAP INTO THEIR "SPECIAL SAUCE"

Sarah told me that if you want to get to the essence of a person's character and the values they hold dear, you need to ask them specific questions:

- Tell me about a time you had to be compassionate at work.

- Tell me about a time you were challenged to be compassionate at work.

- Tell me about a time it was really difficult for you to be compassionate at work.

Keeping interviews more conversational helps you get to the heart of a person vs. the candidate. When it's an interview that sounds scripted, you're not able to expose people to your unique culture or to get a pulse on their response. Other questions that tie back to core values, thinking and cultural principles include:

- Tell me about a time that you were on a team, or a volunteer group, or a project group--could be any kind of a group.

- What was that experience like for you?

- How did you feel working in that particular group?

- Tell me about a time that you were in a group that won or succeeded in an accomplishment.

- Tell me about your role on the team.

- Tell me about a time when your group didn't hit the mark or goal.

- Why do you think things didn't work out in that instance?

People's answers are telling about their character and ability to work with others--so pay attention to how they phrase them. Words help you calibrating whether or not a candidate is a cultural fit. Sarah believes that a candidate who overuses "I" in an interview may be fine to hire as an individual contributor, but not necessarily as a manager. It's also very telling if a candidate fails to answer a question at all, or they struggle, meandering in a roundabout way to find an answer. Not everyone is direct, but when your interviewing, you need to answer every question. To me, not answering a question is a red flag. Answers become much more trustworthy when they are a concrete example of how a candidate has behaved in the past. If I'm interviewing someone and ask them how they would handle a particular situation, I'm concerned if they answer with something along the lines of: "Oh yeah, I believe people should be left on their own to find solutions. I've had great results by not getting into other people's way." That's a great answer, but I won't remember this person until they follow up with, "for example…"

Look for signs other signs of accountability and commitment: concrete examples from past positions, relevant experiences to your company, etc. Is the candidate able to articulate how they can help your company take on its challenges and succeed? Have they invested the effort to research your core mission, values and culture? Can they speak to how their specific skills and background are relevant to the job opening at hand? If not, maybe they lack fire in the belly.

GOLDEN RULE: Your employees are your best hiring tool.

Recently I had the pleasure of sharing a taxi with a hiring manager whose boss has a thing about time. For his boss, being on time shows that employees are passionate about his business. He loves to greet his employees at the door at 8:15am, so he can infuse positive enthusiasm into the start of every day. This type of behavior is obviously not for everyone, but as long as you identify what you're passionate about and you're transparent about it, you'll find the people who share common values.

SPIN ON CULTURES

Culture is collective; it's a team, a family, and a tribe. Culture evolves, and it's not just one individual employee. Every team member contributes to the culture; otherwise, it's called a dictatorship.

Cultures can vary from one extreme to another. Employees may feel like they're locked up in solitary confinement, working for a tyrant, or they might feel like contributing members to the office society. You and the people around you learn by trial and error, by asking questions and by understanding how others around you feel and think. Ask yourself: which organization would you like to work for? For the hiring manager, they need to ask: what does your culture look like? If your culture is something you don't recognize, it's time to change! Take a look inside of yourself and reevaluate. There are a few main types to look out for.

THE SPECTATORS

This is a "wait and see" culture. Employees sit around and wait for things to happen. It's very reactionary—to the market, to financial institutions, to news. In a spectator culture, people depend on the boss to pull the trigger on major decisions. They hold off, sometimes at their own peril, before making a move. Some people like to be told what to do, but then again, this type of culture is not for everybody.

THE WRESTLERS

When two guys are on the mat, twisting arms and slamming each other's bodies into the ground, it's not the friendliest environment. It's a competitive environment. Some might consider it aggressive, but it's not necessarily unhealthy. It's Darwinism--only the strongest survive.

THE BASEBALL TEAM

On a baseball team, everyone has a unique part to play. They might make plays at different times, but everyone has to be alert. If there are no signals or communication, the team can fall apart. The team needs to know if a player is going to steal a base or bunt. Some baseball teams fail while others succeed. It takes an understanding of all of the players' roles and best communication methods to find a good groove in this team.

GREENPEACE CULTURE

Everyone is working towards the good of the whole. There aren't individual incentives but rather, group incentives. Workers want to feel good and they want to feel appreciated. At times it can be tough to criticize someone in this type of environment.

CURIOUS CULTURE

Everyone is exploring beyond the boundaries of, not only the mission statement, but also the possibilities of the company. In the curious culture nothing is off the table because nothing is really seen as impossible. The curious culture won't pursue every thought, but they're just curious enough to push the envelope because they're being encouraged to do so.

Under Steve Jobs, Apple was one of the most creative, exploratory and downright curious companies around. Steve Jobs was all about pushing the boundaries. Now they are just pushing out iPhone after iPhone. Will they be able to take the company to the next level and keep up its innovation track record? Time will tell.

By building a healthy, corporate culture, you are setting up yourself and your company for success. One of my star employees, Toni, (the passionate data-entry person), puts it beautifully: "When you establish values or missions, you feed a person's emotional passion, and so the work becomes an emotional contribution that an individual can make to an organization. Whatever that part may be, whether it's a revenue-generated position or it's a contributor to the processes that make the wheels turn, I think it all comes down to that belief, and that feeling about what your company brings to the table. This energy is set by example. When your senior leaders follow the values and mission of the company, this leadership funnels down to the rest of the team. For example, I say to my own children, I wouldn't ask you to take out the trash if I didn't take out the trash myself. Right? So when I see Erika take out the trash for the business, it validates the fact that she's truly living our values and missions. She's not asking me to go and do anything she wouldn't do herself."

GOLDEN RULE: There might be no "I"
in "team," but there is a "me."

"At least the motivational policy
in the company is clear."

ME AND THE TEAM

There are still some executives who believe that the workplace is for only making money, and that fun, enjoyment and satisfaction are not important factors. They like to work their leaders and team to death and repeat the burn-out process again and again until the end of time. I'm not sure what drives companies to behave this way, but I can assure you that this is not a healthy or successful dynamic. People are not cogs. People are people.

If a person does not feel respected or valued in the workplace, they might not feel comfortable or open enough to even brainstorm. As a result, innovation suffers. A lack of respect stymies production and ultimately the success of the business.

Let's look at NASA. If it weren't for the really good, hard-working people at NASA, would we ever have gone to space? (Or come back to earth for that matter?) NASA is notorious for its "organizational culture." As a federal, science-based agency, it needs to maintain a "culture of excellence" in order to keep its employees focused on the smallest of details, since one little mistake could mean a failed space mission. Yet, even in NASA's somewhat more hierarchical and traditional culture, employees must still rely on one another in collaborative efforts in order to work toward the organization's ultimate aspirations. We might consider the now legendary encounter President John F. Kennedy supposedly had with a janitor at NASA while he was preparing a speech on the Apollo missions. The story goes that when Kennedy asked the janitor what he did, the janitor replied, to Kennedy's surprise, "I'm helping to put a man on the moon." The agency's leaders work hard to instill workers with a sense of purpose, connecting their everyday tasks with the larger mission. Through its organizational culture, NASA employees often report feeling strongly connected to the agency's core objectives and long term goals, regardless of how large or small their everyday contributions turn out to be.[8] Without this shared sense of passion and meaning in their work, would NASA ever have been able to innovate and explore? And where did that collaboration and passion come from in the first place? It came from each individual, the "me" that's in team.

TEAM BUILDING

There is something attractive about a team that is cohesive and on the same page. Strong leaders encourage that collaboration and give employees the autonomy needed for team building. They know that learning the hard way is often the best way. They're right. Here are some handy team-building do's and don'ts:

- Do give your team some wiggle room.

- Don't spoon-feed information.

- Do have employees "look it up" and come to their own conclusions.

- Do play to employees' strengths when assigning tasks.

- Don't set up employees for failure by playing to their weaknesses, however tempting it is to have them stretch.

- Do meet with employees one-on-one to evaluate their role and how they feel about their performance.

- Don't be shy about having a direct conversation.

8 For an in-depth analysis of NASA's leadership, see: Carton, Andrew M. "'I'm Not Mopping the Floors, I'm Putting a Man on the Moon': How NASA Leaders Enhanced the Meaningfulness of Work by Changing the Meaning of Work." *Administrative Science Quarterly* 63, no. 2 (June 1, 2018): 323–69.

- Do make sure you have the right people in the right seats.

- Do encourage employees to discuss what they are proud of, but also what they've learned from their disappointments.

- Do coach employees how to lose so that they are seasoned for success.

DON'T UNDERESTIMATE YOUTH

Ever wonder where Millennials got their reputation? Dishing on the Me Me Me Generation has become a popular sport. We need to keep in mind that previous generations have helped shape the current attitudes of young professionals. A combination of scaffold-parenting and immediate gratification has contributed to the attitudes of cohorts born between 1982 and 2004. When I talk with colleagues about this generation's work/life ethics, I enviably hear that they are the "entitled" generation. But I don't necessarily agree. I think they're the "in-the-moment" generation. Yes, some young people out there feel "entitled." But I grew up with entitled folks––we all did. We need to look at the fact that the newest generation to join the workforce has grown up in the information age—cell phones, live video, chat, snap and slack––which has altered, some might say *enhanced*, the way this generation operates.

Millennials often crave a safe, yet immediate work environment. Years ago, I was planning my daughter's bat mitzvah. Being an environmentally "cool" mom, I decided to send out the invitations via email. Thirty minutes later my daughter comes crying to me saying that no one is coming, no one responded to the evite. OMG, in my day we wrote out the invites and waited four-to-six weeks for responses. You see what I mean about the "in-the-moment" generation?

And yet, I have never met a more passionate generation than the Millennials. In fact, there is a good reason why Millennials differ emotionally from their predecessors, GenY/GenX and the Baby Boomers. Millennials are entering the job market on the heels of the Great Recession, with fewer full-time positions available to them. Perhaps this is why the Millennial generation focuses on work they find fulfilling, rather than making a large paycheck. In the 2015 Allstate/ National Journal Heartland Monitor Poll, respondents were divided into two groups: an older group well into their careers and a younger group just beginning their work journeys. The researchers found that when they asked both groups what their primary concern was during their first job, 57 percent of younger respondents answered that their top priority was to do something they found enjoyable and would make a difference in society while 64 percent of the older generation said making as much money as possible or learning new skills.[9]

Making the world a better place is no empty mantra with the Millennial crowd: any lesser mission wouldn't be fulfilling. Many from this generation would rather work at a company with a humanitarian cause than work for a paycheck. While Millennials might be the "selfie" generation, with all the answers seemingly on their phones, they are also the "selfless" generation. Young professionals look for companies that give to charities and are associated with causes. They look for cultures big on team learning and they value praise. The Millennial generation also has a mix of entitled leaders, followers and creators. But I believe that now more than ever before,

9 White, Gillian B. "Millennials Are Searching for a Different Kind of Career." *CityLab*. June 12, 2015. http://www.citylab.com/work/2015/06/millennials-are-in-search-of-a-different-kind-of-career/395717/.

we have diversity in our workforce. Not just in race, religions and sex, but in belief systems about how to approach work.

Next time you're out with friends, look around. More than likely, they will have similar values, aspirations and ideas. Around the world people create clubs, gangs, associations and other organizations to hang around like-minded people. Being "like-minded" is not only what we think; it's also the power we show to effect change.

Passion resides within our ideas. In terms of hiring, being like-minded and having diversity of thinking are two different things. You can have like-minded goals and values, but might think about things differently and have a difference in opinion.

All organizations need diversity in order to grow and reinvent. The hiring process must address both our immediate concerns and future growth. Too often we forget to ask people about their beliefs and attitudes. When we only focus on skills and bullet points on the résumé, we are endangering our corporate culture.

Two questions I recommend all hiring managers to ask is: "Why do you want to leave your current position?" Then, once you get a firm grasp on their current situation, follow up with: "What needs to be different in your next position?" "Have you tried to address management with how you're feeling?" Why not?" Also ask: "What makes you different from the next candidate with your same credentials?" The hiring manager is looking for someone's humanity, who they are as a person.

GOLDEN RULE: Listen to the new generation,
there is wisdom to be found.

CHAPTER FOUR:

MANAGING DISAPPOINTMENT AND FEAR

I'd venture to say that there isn't a leader out there who hasn't experienced a less than desirable outcome. Maybe an advertising campaign fell flat, someone made a disappointing hire, or a corporate event wound up extremely boring and poorly attended. Be it in business, politics or community, leaders have all have experienced failure.

To quote Bill Clinton: "If you live long enough, you'll make mistakes. But if you learn from them, you'll be a better person. It's how you handle adversity, not how it affects you. The main thing is never quit, never quit, never quit."

My colleagues and I have had our share of letdowns. Once we placed a bookish introvert in a fratty corporate culture (truly sorry). And then there was the smooth talker who turned out to be a diva and unrealistic in his expectations. Or how about the brand guru who was bedazzling with her visionary ideas but took eons to implement them? These are all teachable moments.

Through the ups and downs, we at eTeam have grown spiritually and materially and, I'm happy to report, so have many of the hiring leaders at companies we've had the honor to recruit for over the years. Overcoming disappointment is what makes us strong. It's the ability and freedom to make a mistake. Yes, you heard me, screw-up! But it's also facing the hard facts of a situation that is out of your control.

Everyone has difficult or challenging clients. Recently we had a doozy. What made this particular client, the CEO of an offshore analytics company, less-than-pleasant was his communications with us––rude and screaming, even though we'd successfully recruited two team members for them. We were working on a third placement when we wondered, "Is it worth our time if we keep on feeling demoralized?" Taking a collective sigh, we realized that we needed to resign the account. As a team we learned about disappointment and that sometimes, these experiences are unavoidable. There's nothing shameful about fearing that you will lose the client. Overcoming that fear made us realize that no single client would be so damaging to our business. In the long-run, we had more time to work on new business and devote our energies towards worthy clients. We balanced the emotional bank and felt good about ourselves. Managing disappointment is key to successful living. Life happens and we need to cope with it, learn from it and roll with it.

So why do we feel bad when we mess up? Since most of us set expectations, both reasonable and unattainable, it's easy to get down on yourself when things don't go according to plan. It helps to have a strategy on hand to transform that "down" feeling into motivated action. Think of sales professionals, who are faced with being told "no" on a daily basis. If they aren't getting no's, they are probably not doing their job. Successful sales strategies are constantly changing, because what works with one prospect, doesn't work for all potential clients. Instead of indulging in disappointment, great sales professionals take no and convert into yes.

SETTING EXPECTATIONS

Before you hire anyone, set expectations. I have discovered in recruiting for the past two decades that the most difficult period in people's careers is the first 90 days on a new job. Oftentimes, companies don't have a clear onboarding process and the "newbie" doesn't know protocol or what they are supposed to be doing. Your onboarding process has a direct impact on employee attitudes and on creating winning teams.

Ask yourself after a failure, what was my initial expectation? Did we set realistic goals? The answer is sometimes surprising. Setting expectations is one of the ground rules of business. However, we usually forget this step because setting expectations requires planning and doing homework. Take the salesperson as an example. The best salespeople tend to invest time in researching their prospects before making the pitch. Organizations also need to have effective communications, such as regular meetings to help teams strategize and re-evaluate at each phase of a project. Often, coaching plays a big role in a person's success and how they handle losing. When you lose a pitch to another company, instead of feeling bad about the results, examine the process and use that learning for the next time. Was the presentation designed to make the necessary, immediate impact? What was the initial motivation? Did we take the steps to drive home the unique value of the offering and achieve the desired outcome? Remember that we call it pitching, and the best pitchers in baseball throw a lot of balls to hone their skills.

"What does the company that doesn't
know the meaning of the word
failure need?"

(VOICE IN THE AUDIENCE)
"A dictionary?"

FREEDOM TO FAIL

GOLDEN RULE: I'm never lost, I simply find new places.

You can change a desired outcome if you have a culture that encourages innovation. Innovation comes in two ways: by mistake and by trial and error. Whenever I veer off-piste while traveling, I say that I'm never lost, I simply find new places. And of course, there is the adage: "The road to success is littered with failure." Ask the guys who started Google, Apple and Facebook. Those companies didn't happen overnight, they had to go through a lot of mistakes to get to where they are today.

I recently had a client who was intolerant of mistakes to the point of belittling his staff. My client constantly complained that they couldn't grow their business, that they didn't have enough time to complete client projects. Every person they hired was a failure and "just didn't get it." What the CEO didn't realize was that his rigid management style was the root of the problem. He couldn't or wouldn't understand personal styles. It was his way or the highway.

Innovation comes about by persistent trial and error, just as scientists spend years finding new cures for diseases through consistent experimentation. Many believe that the fastest growing companies have leaders who encourage exploration through trial and error. I can attest to this belief since I often talk with C-suite executives who describe their career as a difficult journey filled with failures. True leaders can withstand disappointment and muster the resilience to achieve success.

HARNESSING OUR FEARS

Fear is a complex emotion. It can be a positive or negative force in our lives, and in certain situations, fear can be paralyzing and destructive. When people feel threatened, their response will be fight or flight. If you push people too far in your company, they might push back or simply walk away from the difficult and scary situation. Employees can become immobilized by fear and consequently, won't take risks or decisive actions. When fear dominates, there is no way forward and the results are detrimental to business. Again, take the salesperson. They can't afford to let fear keep them from picking up the phone.

On the flip side, fear can also be motivating and have a productive effect. In this case, fear becomes the driver and fuels competitiveness. It can make people tap into reserves of determination, imagination and innovation that they didn't know they possessed. Did you ever notice that when the deadline is looming, you start hustling and often become creative? *The pressure is on and I have to kick some butt to hit my monthly goals.* I'm not advocating for things to be left to the last minute; it's just that for some, the real thinking and doing comes in the 11th hour.

Leveraging fear for success goes back to the dawn of human evolution. Back in the caves, our ancestors were afraid of freezing to death, so they built shelters and discovered fire to protect themselves from the elements. Adaptability in the face of adversity is what lets the predator keep hunting and the prey keep escaping and surviving. Fear can be a powerful engine of invention, it's not always bad to be driven by fear.

If you look at IDEO, the spectacularly successful product design and innovation consultancy behind Apple's first mouse, its founder, David Kelley, famously stated that people must reclaim their creative confidence through facing their fears. In a TED talk, Kelley explained that people shy away from creativity because they fear being judged for not saying the right, most creative thing.[10] Using a methodology borrowed from a fellow Stanford Professor, the psychologist Albert Bandura, Kelley explains that he introduces students at the Design School to creativity slowly, allowing them to conquer their fears one step at a time. He also reminds us that, "creativity is something you practice, not just a talent your born with."[11] Practicing creativity means brainstorming ideas for a project right away, no matter how unconventional or impractical they may seem at first. Doing so, according to Kelley, teaches people to resist making judgements about themselves as creatives. Slowly, students can learn how to harness their fears and move forward with ever more creative and innovative ideas.

THE FEARLESS LEADER

There is the famous idea of the "fearless leader," the person who through their personal boldness inspires others to follow them to victory. The most effective leaders, however, are not exactly fearless. Quite the opposite. Leaders have their fair share of sleepless nights. What keeps these people up at night? Failure. The future. Leaders look at themselves and say, "Am I good enough to lead these people? Am I going to be successful?" When a leader looks around and sees

---

10 Kelley, David. *How to Build Your Creative Confidence.* TED, 2012. Video recording. https://www.ted.com/talks/david_kelley_how_to_build_your_creative_confidence.
11 Kelley, David, and Tom Kelley. "Reclaim Your Creative Confidence." *Harvard Business Review* 90, no. 12 (December 2012): 115–18.

companies from Ringling Bros. Circus to Sears teetering on the edge and going out of business they might wonder if they're next.

A great leader understands their employees, but that understanding comes, in part, from acknowledging their own psychology. They put emotions such as fear in context and understand the consequences. It doesn't do good to pretend that a big decision isn't a serious matter, but a leader also can't let fear debilitate them, rather, it has to galvanize them. When people are counting on you, or looking to you for guidance, you can't shrink from that moment. That's why not everyone is cut out for leadership. Not everyone can understand their fear, and ultimately channel this strong emotion.

People don't like failure, especially leaders. They don't like rejection either. They want to belong and, most importantly, receive praise. Therefore it stands to reason that we should always challenge ourselves to get out of our comfort zone. The bottom line is that we worked at discovering fire because waiting for lightning to strike was just too risky a strategy.

People often amplify their fears, allowing them grow out of proportion. If you're the leader, it's important to help your team members figure out what they're afraid of. Is it failure? Is it being rejected? As a leader, you need your employees to trust you to put them in situations where they can succeed. Like an army going into battle, harnessing fear into motivation can unite people and achieve something bigger than the individual.

Harnessing and managing fear comes down to listening: to your team, to your client and ultimately to some combination of your brain and your gut. How you interpret the fears of those around you will help you figure out the right way forward. Listen closely and you'll discover that your client fears costs vs. gains--or maybe that an employee's fear of making a mistake is inhibiting their ability to do their job. If you remain aware and forthcoming, you're open to a whole new set of solutions. Look at fear head on and you may just invent, create and inspire.

CHAPTER FIVE:

IN THE BEGINNING

Like any other major decision in life, such as deciding to live together or to have a child, hiring a new employee is a process. Unfortunately, there is no such thing as the perfect husband/wife/significant other, nor will a flawless employee simply appear at your door. Don't go into the hiring process expecting a quick, custom-made fix. These things take time to work their magic.

RECRUITING 3RS

I believe in the three Rs of business: referral, research and relevance.

Referral is the external validation process through which new candidates come into the process. Relevance is discovery of personality and relevant skills and how they match with culture, needed skills and goals. Research the referred candidate's background to understand their history, reach out to your network for opinions about the candidate.

A well planned hiring process creates a decision map.

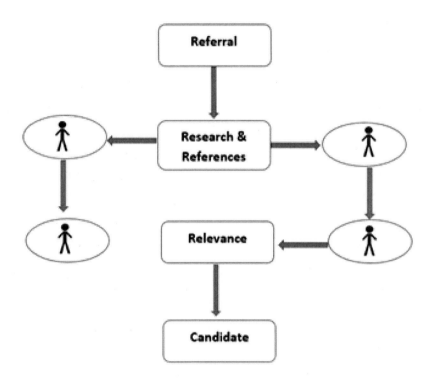

While we can analyze and strategize all night long, you also need to feel your gut. I believe instinct is the special sauce––to me, ignoring our emotional intelligence is akin to eating without taste buds. But how do you know when to trust your intuition and when to ignore it? You will inevitably make hiring mistakes, but creating and following a plan, such as the 3Rs will help set you on a solid path to hiring success.

THE ICEBREAKER

When starting your search for the perfect candidate, it can be scary to pick up the phone and call someone cold. It helps to have some icebreaker questions. The first thing I ask a candidate is, "Do you have a moment?" or, "You don't know me, but after a nanosecond we'll be the best of friends". A sense of humor can go a long way. It relaxes people, kicks off their endorphins and puts them in an open frame of mind. Don't take yourself too seriously and don't take it personally when you don't get an immediate response. People are busy! Plus, having a sense of humor about yourself frees up your mind and might help to relieve your anxiety about the situation.

Be prepared for the unexpected. Most candidates will say, "Well, I'm already happy." Don't stop probing about their current state. Happy, successful people are the best candidates. In fact, I only talk to happy people. Follow up with, "Great, what makes you happy?" Every happy person has an answer to, "What would make you happier?" They may say, "You know what? Really, nothing right now." Which is your cue to go, "God bless you, man, I love that. Do you mind if I call you back just to make sure you keep on being happy?" There are those people who are never going to budge, and that's also fine.

WHAT MAKES SOMEONE OPEN UP?

People don't have to talk to me, and if I wasn't passionate or excited about my job, no one would want to talk to me. What helps me is that I approach every conversation like I'm learning something new from an old friend. I truly want to understand candidates' dreams, desires and hopes for that next step. I'm not serving a candidate what's on my menu (my agenda, the job description, etc.), rather, I have real conversations with people in which I try to understand their interests, needs, passions and what environment is truly the best fit for the candidate.

Wouldn't it be great if we could go to a restaurant and the chef came out and announced, "What would you love to eat today?" I'm not saying I can deliver the exact menu or have the perfect job for you, but I care about how people feel and I want candidates to feel deeply passionate about their career. Both hiring managers and candidates need to match their passions.

GOLDEN RULE: In hiring, there is no room for unrequited love!

INTEGRITY: WHAT DOES IT MEAN TO YOU?

It's a basic question that can be interpreted as, "Why should somebody work with me?" For starters, trust is a must. The ability to build a genuine relationship through listening is the starting block for trust between people. I'm not necessarily always ready with an answer, but I'm all ears and ready to learn more. I'm responsible and hold myself and my colleagues to the highest bar. Through an initial discussion, during which we probe our clients for clues into their working style, their wants and needs, we sometimes realize our company is not the right solution to our client's needs.

I believe in mutual respect, meaning, I stand up for the right thing, which may not include a monetary gain. Bottom line is, always be authentic––treat people how you want to be treated. Personally, I never have to look over my shoulder and can go to sleep at night knowing that I did my honest best.

WHY SHOULD I WORK FOR YOU?

It makes perfect sense that you should love what you do, because you probably spend most of your time working. Personally, I enjoy the diversity of work cultures, strategies and missions that the recruitment industry affords me. Each client has their own unique ideas, operating procedures and growth strategies, but what they all have in common is that their success comes down to their people.

Hiring managers need to ask, "Why is someone going to come work for us?" Unless you already have the top performers knocking down your doors, you will need to articulate your values and be able to answer, "Why are we a great company?"

If you're a hiring manager able to give a unique value proposition, can you articulate what's appealing about your culture? Most hiring managers I meet think their company is the best place to work. They're entitled. Just as I'm entitled to respectfully disagree. All too often, the same people are unable to describe their company's culture. Some can't even tell me what differentiates them in the marketplace. And yet, the answers to these seemingly simple questions are the essential brand DNA and what sets them apart from the pack.

> **GOLDEN RULE:** Before you look outside
> for talent, look inside for the fire.

Look, we all have bad days. Sometimes passion wanes. Many people, at some point in their career, and for that matter, their personal lives, need to find ways to reignite their passion. Back in the day, people worked because they had to feed their families. Job satisfaction didn't top the list; in fact it wasn't part of the equation. Attitudes toward work have long since shifted to a more holistic approach. Nowadays the pursuit of career happiness is all but an inalienable right. I have seen time and time again the frustration that occurs when we hire people who aren't the right fit. Hiring managers don't get enjoyment out of firing people any more than people relish going to a job they dread. It's not life-fulfilling and it's not healthy.

"Some companies take the principle of hire slowly, fire quickly more seriously than others."

HIRE SLOWLY, FIRE QUICKLY

Take your time to date potential employees. Explore each other carefully. I had a client, Tacori, the fine jewelry company out on the West Coast, that flew in a very accomplished man named Martin to interview and waited eight months to make a final decision. While eight months might sound like a call for concern, they ultimately hired Martin. Think about it, you might get stuck with this person for years! Hopefully, the candidate is the kind of person you'll want to get stuck with for the long haul.

I get really nervous when my clients say, "I'm really in a rush. I need to fill this role. How quickly can you do it?" That's not the question they should be asking. What they should be asking is, "How long does it take to vet somebody and to really understand what they're looking for? How long does it take to match passionate people to my culture?" I try to avoid working with clients who rush the process. A rushed process is not a successful process. They should also be asking themselves, "What is my culture and will this person be a valuable team member?" If you don't know, you will most likely end up firing that person.

There are many people who have hired the wrong person and then feel responsible for that hiring. They might have to take part of responsibility, but that doesn't mean they shouldn't have a conversation with the candidate when it is time to move on. As human beings, we tend to hope things will work out with a new hire and that is just not a good strategy. Most people can learn new skills or your way of business. But if they're not the right cultural fit, you can't make them fit. In other words, you can't put a square peg in a round hole. What you're doing by not firing someone quickly is prolonging the agony for you and the person you hired. Ultimately, it will negatively impact your culture and your own job performance.

RÉSUMÉ CLUES

These days résumés look like checkerboards, filled with positions and lots of hopping around. It's not unusual for the longest tenure to be five years. In this world of "job shifters," it's difficult to hire people who give a sh*t. So what's a company to do? If you're looking to hire people who have demonstrated accountability and commitment—and you are—the résumé is a good place to start.

Looking at a résumé is like an Easter egg hunt. I look to see when and where the candidate graduated school. Yes, dates are important because it speaks to tenure and experience. Then I look at the places they worked and the length of time they worked at each place. How long someone stuck around shows me if they saw real progress.

Next, I look at what they don't have on their résumé. If they're speaking in company-ese (the language of their current company), I tend to gloss over it. Hint: nobody outside of your company understands that language.

I look for clear and concise communication. Is the person articulate? Can they express accomplishments in a few sentences? Whether it's creating, discovering, selling, or contributing, every piece of experience must be conveyed in a concise manner. You're not writing a book here.

When I see résumés that read; one-year, one-year, one-year, those tend to send up red flags for hiring managers. I often put those résumés in the trash can. I'm okay with a couple of one-years, but if you have a short career of five years and it's one-year, one-year, one-year after that, unless every time you go to a company, it's been sold and you've made a million dollars, I'm going to have to question your accountability. You didn't stay long enough to accomplish anything. Even if you created something, did you stay to figure out if your plan worked? If the information you provided was valid, and you're an analytics person, or a salesperson, did you stay long enough to make an impact? What was that impact? Don't bullshit me with, "I had a million dollars in the pipeline." People aren't interested in pipelines. They're interested in bottom-line results.

At the same time, sometimes I meet people who have stable backgrounds with long tenures at companies and for whatever reason, they moved onto a new job, only to realize, "Oh sh*t, I made a mistake." It may take them a couple of short tenure positions to find their groove again.

I advise hiring managers to focus more on accountability than the number of positions. Did the candidate have a track record of staying and succeeding at a company for any reasonable amount of time? Many candidates have good, solid reasons why something didn't last longer: the company went out of business, the boss that hired them was fired or left and they went with him or her, or the company just totally changed after the management changed... I could go on and on. But, if you're a consistent job-hopper, my antenna goes up.

"Why do I think you lied on your W2? You misspelled W2."

HOW MUCH TRUTH IS IN THE RÉSUMÉ?

I don't find that many people lie on their résumés these days. Pre-LinkedIn days, people exaggerated and sometimes fibbed, but in the age of transparency it's easy to check up on accuracy. I have come across people who have inconsistencies with their social media and their résumé and they need to explain it. If they can't, they're just not believable and probably not the best hire.

Hiring managers ask me all the time, "What do people exaggerate about?" Often people inflate their salary. Understand that people are only human (newsflash), so cut candidates a break. You can tell them that during the process, you will require a W2 or some proof of earnings. At the same time, when we're job hunting or hunting for talent, I beleive we place too much emphasis on the monetary side. In fact laws have changed in many states, including New York, Rhode Island, Massachusetts, Pennsylvania and California, making it illegal to ask for previous W2s. This type of change is a good thing, as its designed to prevent discrimination, especially for women and minority groups. That said, it's up to you to determine reliability through the interviewing process.

Another résumé point people often exaggerate is their accomplishments. For the most part, people are being up front but as humans we tend to exaggerate a little. That said, résumés should be used simply to start the conversation. You will actually find out more about the person once you start interviewing them.

GOLDEN RULE: Don't discuss the size
of the ring until you fall in love

"Ivy league school? There were a
lot of weeds, some of them might
have been ivy."

WHY ARE WE INFLUENCED BY
SCHOOL STEREOTYPES?

The importance of a degree depends on many factors. I'm a graduate of the 'School of Hard Knocks' and in learning-as-you-go. Work experience is irreplaceable. Besides, not everybody's fortunate to have gone to college. Of course, there are professions such as medicine, engineering and microbiology where the degree and, often, the pedigree are important. In certain professions, the degree isn't just an education: it confers a sense of belonging to the same tribe, club or sorority/fraternity.

Look at the folks at NASA. A lot of them come from MIT, Stanford, Harvard, Princeton and Yale, and this distinction is important to them. Why? Because people love being with like-minded people. I advise Millennials today: "When you look on social media for opportunities, search for people who graduated from your school, because the alumni tend to want to help you. It's your club. It's your tribe. If you study engineering, go look up the engineering guys that went to your university and reach out to them."

There are many assumptions behind the issue of the "right" schooling, but in the job hunt, it comes down to what's important to the hiring manager. I'll give you an example.

A couple of years ago, I was recruiting for a licensing company and I had already signed the retainer agreement. I met with the hiring team, and while we were sitting at their conference table, getting to know the current employees at the company, I realized the more we talked how important it was to them that the new hire come from an Ivy League school. I didn't understand why, because the job just didn't require that level of 'Ivy' sophistication. I asked one of the women, "Why is school pedigree so important?" She said to me, as if it was obvious, "Well, I went to an Ivy League school." Aha! I thought. It's the club. "I only hire people from the Ivy League," she said. I told her, "I just want to let you know, Helen, that I didn't go to an Ivy League school. In fact, I don't even have a four-year degree. I don't know how that makes you feel, but I wanted to be very transparent with you." I could tell she was a little uncomfortable with how direct I was being.

Helen didn't say anything immediately. After we completed a successful search, she came to me and told me, "You know, I really learned a valuable lesson: my criteria wasn't aligned with my goals. You made me realize I was limiting the search. I really like the fact that you were so transparent with me about your education. Based on our conversation, I rethought my hiring criteria in relation to the job requirements. Thank you."

They wound up not hiring someone from an Ivy League school, but loving the person they did hire. That's the thing about hiring: when you bring someone aboard, you're telling them you believe in their passion and goals. Sometimes an Ivy League education is warranted for the kind of drive a position requires. Don't let your preconceived vision of candidates from high-powered schools limit your decision-making.

CHAPTER SIX:

WHAT'S YOUR PROCESS?

When it comes to hiring, many hiring managers believe they already have a strategic process in place, but when asked *why* they are looking to hire, they typically base their answers on immediate needs, instead of on the future of the organization. Their decision to hire is usually a reaction to new or lost business and/or retention issues, rather than planning for growth. Hiring to fill a hole is anything but strategic.

There are three key types of hiring in business: strategic, opportunistic and reactive. Knowing when and how to differentiate between them can mean the difference between high performance and underwhelming return on investment (ROI).

STRATEGIC HIRING

Strategic hiring is part of your long-term vision. It's not about where you are today, it's where you want to be tomorrow, and who is going to be on your proverbial bus. Strategic hiring needs to be an integral part of your business planning process and it needs to be intentional.

As you look carefully at the markets you intend to enter, expand in or exit, be sure to define the pivotal strategies required to enhance your market share and the resources available within the firm. If the talent is not available in-house, you'll need to define what skills, knowledge and attributes you need to achieve specific outcomes. I want to understand, "What's the performance expectation? What do you need a person to do? What do you want them to achieve? And how should they go about it?"

Having clear intent and purpose around roles and responsibilities drives strategic hiring. When you're ready to explore the market, don't leave it up to an inexperienced manager who doesn't understand your business needs and goals or, more broadly, the intricacies of today's demanding skill sets. Hiring talent is usually your most costly investment and if you're going to rely on your junior staffers, at least help them prepare a list of qualifications including position responsibilities, education, years of experience, technical or business strengths, requirements and salary range.

Investing in today's uncertain world of economic ups and downs requires leaders to pay attention to their growth strategy. When hiring your top performers, it's equally important to invest in their success. Bruce Budkofsky, Vice President of Sales at a media company, explained to me once that he implements practices he personally believes in to make the most of his talent investment. He told me, "I recognize I'm paying someone for their skills and their past performance regarding accomplishments. However, the more I can invest in them through training and helping them build their own relationships in the marketplace––by sending them to conferences or by having them join different associations and important boards––the better their chances of success."

Strategic hiring is especially important when your company is experiencing an economic downturn. We all hear about massive layoffs and cost cutting. I often fear, however, that trimming the bottom line doesn't always consider the top line. While some talent trimming is reactionary (e.g., "Hey, we've hit a blip in productivity or performance in the business and we must shrink down,") people too often get cut without management being strategic about it. While you are trimming down, there's still an opportunity to think ahead. There are business and market cycles and two years from now things could change, so how are you going to calibrate and modify your business practices to be able to retain and grow talent?

OPPORTUNISTIC HIRING

Make it a point to meet outstanding candidates, the achievers and rock stars. These stellar candidates are commonly passed over. Why? It might be because they don't fit the open job spec or because the person recruiting has a narrow understanding of the profile and is unable to see their value. Opportunistic hiring is about pinpointing those rock stars, those gems you meet when you're not looking for anyone in particular. Maybe you're walking along the beach, or out shopping when you meet someone extraordinary and you choose to hire that person instinctively, in hopes that they can bring valuable skills to your team. Many of these rainmakers can also bring clients with them, find opportunities most never knew existed and keep other people's plates full by bringing new insights and project ideas. If you're not thinking strategically and/or opportunistically, you're at a disadvantage.

Not only will your current business benefit from a team of multi-talented, emerging stars, your growth prospects also stand to dramatically improve. With your employee brand clearly laid out, you will be able to attract the best people to your door. Before you embark on a human resources strategy, you must have a consistent philosophy about how you will manage your staff. Although many leaders try to keep costs down, don't cut corners on new hire screening and selection tools.

I once had the pleasure of speaking with Keenan Beasley, Co-founder and Managing Director of BLK BOX (formerly known as The Strategy Collective), a boutique, data-driven marketing agency. I asked Keenan if he ever hired opportunistically. "Absolutely!" he gushed. "A producer I met was a rock star. I had seen his work with other agencies. We were having a conversation and I didn't have a role available, but when he said he was interested in joining, I jumped on it and brought him in. I knew from a strategic standpoint the value of production for our group, so that's an investment we were willing to make on an individual because we know that returns will be there."

Keenan is a rare breed of entrepreneurial leaders who, "doesn't hire just positions; [he] hires people who are poly-disciplined." Keenan can't afford to hire narrow-minded, one-trick ponies. He doesn't just hire "a copywriter or a designer." As he puts it, "Everyone who works here creates, everyone is a creator." Keenan's method of opportunistic hiring allows him to spot those gems in everyday interactions.

REACTIVE HIRING

Reactive hiring is when hiring managers react to company needs rather than plan for them. Most of us are privy to the process of reactive hiring, if not guilty of it, ourselves.

Senior executives often find themselves in desperate straits because, while their key people are overworked or behind schedule, their client nevertheless expects the schedule to be maintained. Only when they are in crisis mode do they alert the human resource team and the recruiting process begins.

As we've discussed, it takes time to hire key talent. While in the reactive mode, we have the tendency to hire someone to fill an immediate need and too often rush the process or potentially ignore someone who might bring more value to the firm in the long-run. There will always be reactive recruiting and at times reacting quickly is essential, however, I would venture to say that strategic and opportunistic hiring are much more solid approaches to hiring.

What can leaders do to ensure that they hire only essential talent? The question really is about essential people. If your hires are not adding value, then why are they working at your company? A hiring manager's number one job is to increase the number of market leaders, client leaders and top-notch doers to attract new clients and secure more of your existing clients' business.

TODAY'S LEADERS ON RECRUITING PRACTICES

Hiring is an essential part of your vision. Therefore, I recommend you bring in your most respected leaders at your company and have them be part of your plan. Define a vision and communicate that vision to your human resources employees. Evolving a high-performance organization is difficult, but the payoff is huge. By focusing on the quality of people, rather than on body count, you not only increase your company's profits, you develop a corporate culture that reflects your business vision.

What are the current hiring measuring sticks other than leadership vision and values, mission and culture? I was curious about how some of today's iconic leaders define standards.

Mark Zuckerberg, Facebook CEO, believes that, "a candidate's attitude toward their work matters more than their skills." Zuckerberg says he "will only hire someone to work directly for me if I would work for that person."[12] Of course, Zuckerberg is a visionary thinker and not a reactionary hiring executive. He wants his team to hire the right people and encourages them to interview even when they don't have an opening, because he understands that talent doesn't stand still.

Richard Branson, Virgin Group Founder and CEO, believes, "company culture is paramount to a successful company" and that "personality is the key." Per Branson, "If you can find people who are fun, friendly, caring and love helping others, you are onto a winner." He goes on to say that, "some managers get hung up on qualifications. I only look at them after everything else." However, Branson embraces diversity because he understands that "somebody who thinks a little differently can help to see problems as opportunities and inspire creative energy within a group. Some of the best people we've ever hired didn't seem to fit in at first, but proved to be indispensable over time."[13]

12 Larssen, Adrian Granzella. "Mark Zuckerberg's #1 Hiring Rule (and What You Can Learn From It)." *The Muse*, March 13, 2015. https://www.themuse.com/advice/mark-zuckerbergs-1-hiring-rule-and-what-you-can-learn-from-it.
13 Branson, Richard. "How I Hire: Focus On Personality." LinkedIn, September 23, 2013. https://www.linkedin.com/pulse/20130923230007-204068115-how-i-hire-focus-on-personality/

Tim Brown, IDEO CEO, believes, "emotional intelligence is paramount, and for good reason." Brown explains: "IDEO's stock in trade is creativity, collaboration and human-centered innovation. The success of our company depends upon hiring people who are not only smart and talented, but who also have great emotional intelligence. We look for insatiable curiosity, irrepressible optimism, deep empathy and those who play well with others," he wrote in a LinkedIn post. Brown says he looks for five specific qualities in candidates:

1. They say "we" more than "I."

2. They talk about failures, not just wins.

3. They've spent time teaching as well as learning.

4. They're nice to the receptionist.

5. The candidate has done more than just send in a résumé. They've also "taken creative license and gone the extra mile to demonstrate their capabilities and passion."[14]

Zuckerberg, Branson and Brown are a few of the many leaders thinking strategically about how to build up their teams, all with different approaches. There are, however, a few common threads to successful, strategic hiring.

---

14 Brown, Tim. "How I Hire: 5 Tips for Landing a Job at IDEO." LinkedIn. September 24, 2013. https://www.linkedin.com/pulse/20130924105210-10842349-how-i-hire-5-tips-for-landing-a-job-at-ideo/.

"Yes we appreciate you've been reaping for all eternity, but do you have any other skills?"

THE STRATEGIC HIRING PROCESS—WHAT TO CONSIDER.

1. **Agree on Expectations**

   Once a company determines that it needs to make a new hire, management must first establish responsibilities, accountabilities and goals for the position. This sounds obvious, but it's always good to gut-check different people in the organization.

2. **Internal Communication**

   Create an interview team that designs the hiring process, such as who conducts an interview, which questions to ask and what style and demeanor the team should project. The interview team sets the logics, interview order and techniques, such as group, situational or presentation interview. Remember, your interview team represents your values and culture.

3. **Competitors and Internal Referrals**

   Where to begin looking for top talent to recruit? Remember the first of the 3Rs--referrals--so ask your best employees for their recommendations. The other avenue is raiding the competition. Top candidates are likely working, and if they aren't working for you, they're probably working for your competitors. These super-achievers have little time to interview. It's important to be prepared and remember to ask them, "What would make you happier?" Also tell the story of why you work at your own company, tying into the conversation your company's vision and strategy.

Be prepared to explain how the opportunity could present advancement, more money, a better lifestyle and/or a greater challenge. Always be prepared with open-ended questions. You need better insight into a prospect's career objectives, personality characteristics and skill sets, and the only way to find out is to listen.

4. **Think Outside the Box**

After you've exhausted your network, put together a target list of companies to recruit from. Usually it will be direct competitors, but many times it is related businesses—don't be afraid to think outside your own industry! Of course, there are always headhunters, who have diverse databases and perspectives.

5. **Interview tools**

At eTeam, we subscribe to the philosophy of "behavioral interviewing." Since you already know a candidate's history from their résumé, now you want to know how their behavior helped to manifest their goals. Behavioral interviewing allows an interviewer to understand the candidate's way of thinking. This technique is based on the premise that past performance in a similar situation is the most accurate predictor of future performance.

Behavioral interview questions usually ask the "how" and "why" while challenging the candidate to describe a situation. Here are some of my favorite interview questions:

- What's your definition of multitasking? Provide an example of how you manage your time.

- What do you love to do and how have you shared (teaching moments) your passion with others?

- Who is your mentor and what value did you get from your relationship?

- Describe a situation where you were not successful. What hampered your success? And what did you learn from this experience?

- What's missing from your current situation that you are looking to change in a new position and how have you tried to bring about change?

It's important to understand that there are no right or wrong answers in a behavioral interview. Listen and look for effective communication and thought leadership skills. Do they speak your language? Cultural fit can often be determined by how someone speaks. The people who usually work out in your company are the people who sound like your company. A successful behavioral interview should be able to determine:

- How well a candidate will fit into an organization.

- How they handle stress.

- A candidate's creative, strategic, operational abilities, etc.

- Whether the candidate demonstrates leadership potential.

- Whether the candidate is a team player or lone wolf.

6. **Smile, No Matter What**

As I said earlier, it's important to sell each candidate on the position, the vision and the culture of the company, regardless of the outcome. Why? Simple. It's a small world, and candidates always talk to their friends and co-workers and write about you on social media. Even if it's clear a candidate won't work out, the interview process should always be positive.

Part of the interview team's job is to help create positive buzz in the industry. In recruiting and networking, it's typical that top candidates know others who could fit into the role. Make sure the door is always open.

7. **The Obvious and the Basic
(Yet We Don't Always Remember To…)**

Be personable. Relate to the candidates within their world and not just within yours.

Be cultural. Let them know what sets your firm apart from the pack. Provide examples of how your company is a collection of unique and talented individuals.

Be a listener. Engage candidates by letting them interview you as part of the conversation. Worthy candidates come to the table with great questions.

Be open. Discuss how candidates can contribute and accomplish big-picture goals that work towards the firm's vision. Also discuss where you see opportunities for improvement.

Be visionary. Let candidates see your passion for pursuing the firm's vision. People are looking for more than just a job or single project.

Successful companies recruit through their most visionary leaders. Your clients are attracted to them, and potential staff will be, too. It's not something to be treated cavalierly, and it's not something to be delegated. Filling your company with quality people requires a streamlined process for identifying, interviewing and signing top candidates.

GOLDEN RULE: Hiring should start with your leaders

CHAPTER SEVEN:

HOW DO I FIND PEOPLE WHO GIVE A SH*T?

IF YOU COULD WAVE A MAGIC WAND, WHAT WOULD YOU CHANGE?

When getting to know my clients, I try to determine if eTeam if our methodology their style? Is our personality right for them? I also look at whether they're a good fit with us. What gets them excited? Understanding the client's vision is of paramount importance in professional matchmaking. Of course, I want to understand their mission, values, what's working, and what's not working. Inspiring others isn't easy. What does it take? I believe inspiration comes from loving what you do. But what if you don't know what you love or what you would change? How can you exhilarate others?

Questions of purpose often come up with those right out of school. For example, I was coaching a recent college grad who had earned a mechanical engineering degree, but for the life of him he didn't know what he wanted to do. He got a job at a construction company (he hates it) doing estimating and not mechanical engineering. As a result, he's currently taking a hard look at what he wants. Though it wasn't exactly what he studied, I remind him that he's learned a unique skill while working at the construction company. Now the question is: "How do I apply my new skills and combine it with my love of engineering to a new position and/ or industry?" I advise him that what's in front of you now may be a great gift in the long-term. It also may not be a gift you ever open, and that's ok, the skills you learn now are important nonetheless.

It's not just kids out of college. I've meet successful people, doctors, lawyers and CEOs who still grapple with their career choices. For instance, I once met a former doctor through a friend's birthday party named Larry. After years of practicing medicine, Larry decided that what he really wanted to do was become an art dealer. Having saved for years, he could afford to drop everything to pursue his real passion. It wasn't always an easy transition. Larry had to rent a small room downtown and eventually, he opened up a cramped gallery showcasing. It wasn't ideal, but Larry was positively in love with his new career. He's one of the lucky few who transformed his hobby into a job he's passionate about.

We all have hobbies that we keep on the back burners of our lives, waiting for the day to explore them further. What if you can't afford to quit your career to take up a new one? Let's be real, most of us can't do what my doctor friend did. What would it take to rededicate yourself to your current field? I believe that you should try to fall in love again, if you can. I'm not an expert, but I have been with the same man for 28+ years and counting, so I know a thing or two about re-lighting the fire. Igniting your passions is a two-way street, you need to be able to give yourself the ability to fall in love with your current job while keeping open the possibility of other opportunities. Our careers are like a series of relationships and must constantly be examined and re-ignited. Start writing, giving back, joining an organization or becoming a board member. Start investigating new methods in your industry, go back to school or better yet, teach.

WHO DO YOU ADMIRE?

Thanks for asking. I've admired many women who started nowhere and wound up building an empire. Right up there is Sara Blakely, founder of Spanx, the youngest self-made female billionaire in America. Sara believes "it's important to be willing to make mistakes. The worst thing that can happen is you become memorable." I constantly remind myself about Sara's mantra when building my business, because I make mistakes all the time. Learning, always learning!

A few years back, while interviewing a CEO candidate for a search, I asked, "Who most influenced you in business?" My candidate got a little indignant. "You've got to be kidding! That's a very soft and fuzzy question. What kind of search are we talking about?"

"Yes, it is a soft and fuzzy question because I want to know who you are as a person," I retorted back to him. "My client could have asked a skill-set question, but they really wanted to ask the name of the person you most admired in business, because they wanted to understand your values." If we don't understand the long-term vision, we can't even begin to speak about technicalities.

The answer to this question could be anyone, your father, your mother, your child. The answers to these "soft and fuzzy questions" tell a lot about people, because inspiration is personal, and inspiration drives change.

GOLDEN RULE: Hire for change

The foremost reason a client is looking for somebody is because they either have an issue that they are trying to resolve, or they have something that's great that they want to grow. You don't hire people to stay stagnant; you don't hire people to do the status quo. You might hire strategically, opportunistically or reactively. Whatever your hiring strategy is, you are trying to make a positive change, not keep the status quo.

Recently I was asked to meet the former CEO of the fashion company, which has since closed its doors. The first thing I noticed when walking around the office was that the employees were dressed horribly (they all wore flip-flops––my pet peeve). I had even gone out and bought a shirt from one of the company's stores to wear for the meeting, ready to discuss the brand, yet there was no one around to connect with on the matter. Furthermore, there was an open desk floor plan, but the mood around the office was completely quiet and somber. No one spoke to each other or socialized. I thought, "Isn't fashion supposed to be fun and chic?" I immediately understood why they were not resonating in today's marketplace. No one was engaged and no one was resonating with the brand. How can you expect to relay the company mission to your customers if you can't do it amongst your coworkers? When you're not engaged, you can't understand trends, you can't adapt to the changes in the market and you can't connected with your constituencies.

In the end, I didn't take the assignment, not because there were lots of inherent problems, but because the CEO couldn't get his employees passionate about the brand themselves. He was not the role model to admire. I wouldn't feel right about recruiting for the status quo.

DO YOUR RESEARCH

Discovering new facts about organizations and potential hires is not just about talking to the hiring person or organization. It's not a good idea to rely solely on the internet and websites. I always encourage people, "You can talk to me and find out what I'm about. Then I want you to talk to Joan, eTeam's President, and find out what she thinks. Next, talk to my marketing person, Tim, and find out what I'm about. After that I want you to call a client and get their perspective." With every viewpoint, you get another glimpse into someone's persona or culture.

I guarantee you're going to get four different stories from four different people, all of which will be true. We all listen and experience differently. Which is why writing a position spec is so important.

GET ON THE SAME PAGE

Your position spec serves as your marketing document, and it's an interpretation of whom you need to hire and what they need to accomplish. The spec should be realistic and everybody has to agree on it. That means it has to make sense to your recruiting manager, who's going out there and calling candidates. Whether you are working with an internal recruiter or an outside headhunter, if you don't know what you're looking for, how will you find them?

The position spec must include the brand essence of the company. Most job specs don't clearly state the company's mission. It should include something that explains this: here's why you should work for us!

NARROWING THE FIELD

Now you've contacted a number of candidates and you have a good list. Instead of finding more candidates, it's time to narrow the field. It's not logical to speak with a ton of people after your initial vetting process. How on earth would you find the time to determine who gives a sh*t?

I approach every conversation with the same goal: getting to know you. My staff laughs at me because I like to sing "Getting to Know You" from *The King and I* around the office. In learning about the candidate, there can be no prefab script. Lose the agenda and make it about the other person, because it's going to be about the other person anyway.

If you start out all ears, it's much more strategic. For one thing, time is of the essence and you don't want to waste it. If you're not feeling what you need to feel, not hearing what you need to hear, you should cut it short and move onto the next candidate. Asking questions makes your job easier than coming up with the answers.

When we think about hiring, we think of the interviewing process. But let's think about interviewing as dating. The process is the same. You speak with prospective matches on the phone, you meet them in person and you ask them questions. Remember, there are no wrong or right answers to these types of questions. My top five:

- Whom do you admire in business today?

- What's the first thing you do when you come to work?

- What's the last thing you do before leaving work?

- Outside of work, what are you good at?

- Prioritize your day for me.

It doesn't matter if you ask five or 20 questions, as long as they really matter to you. Are they on the same page as you? Do they have the same passions? Do they feel and look like your team? Will they bring new thinking and energy?

I typically ask candidates, "What are your life's greatest accomplishments?" Often they hesitate, because they think it's a trick question. "Well is that at work or at home?" they'll ask. Hint: it's your answer, so it could be at work or at home, depending on your passion. If your kids are your ecstasy, who's to tell you it should be spreadsheets?

Many years ago, I was talking to a beautiful young African-American woman, and I asked her, "Cynthia what's your greatest life accomplishment?" She looked at me and said, "Me." I was taken aback. "What do you mean, you?" I asked. She told me, "Well Erika, I've got to tell you I went to Harvard on a full scholarship. I was very proud of myself at that time. Very few African-Americans went to Harvard. I graduated and I was about to go to Harvard Business School when my dad, who ran our family business, had a heart attack. Somebody had to take over the business. I got it into really good shape so that when my dad, thank God, got better, I was able to hand it back to him. I went back to Harvard and got my MBA."

For me, Cynthia's response was a total wow. It was unusually impassioned and honest and it revealed her essence.

I once had a gentleman say to me, "My greatest accomplishment was taking my sailboat around the world for a year. I went through storms and hurricanes and tsunamis, and I not only survived it all, I came out the other side a different person. I learned that I can rely on myself. And I developed an appreciation of not just my life, but of other people's lives. It changed my perspective on what it means to be human."

Asking heartfelt answers that speak to culture helps narrow down the field, and what's left are people you feel confident can do the job and give a sh*t.

GOLDEN RULE: Talk the same language

PULL THE PLUG ON THE CANDIDATE

I have a favorite scene in the movie *Philadelphia* where Jason Robards is looking at Tom Hanks' AIDS patient, who was fired from his firm. Roberts starts to use legalese when he addresses the jury. The camera pans, and we see the jury's eyes glazing over as they become disengaged. We all glaze over when we can't understand someone. Stop talking in your current company's dialect. Aside from the people you work with, no one understands you. You need to paint a picture with details and tell a passionate story your audience understands.

A great example of a candidate disconnecting during the process was a CMO search in Washington, DC for a technology company. Both my team and the client agreed Denise was fabulous, and she got through the first phase of the recruitment process with flying colors. Denise was a catch with phone screens and in-person interviews. When she got to the written portion, she shot herself in the foot. Instead of writing about her track record of success and the strategies she innovated to achieve them, she took us on a slog through the technical aspects of her company. Her answers were couched in company jargon and she lost us all.

I pulled the candidate. The first thing my client said to me was, "Why did you pull Denise? She's great! We love her background. She interviewed great, so why is she out of the running?" I was quick to respond, "I pulled Denise because she didn't pass the written portion of the conversation."

After reading the interview my client was dumbfounded, but she still really wanted this candidate. We went back to Denise and asked her to rewrite the assignment. She said, "No, I think I did a great job." I said, "Fair enough, I will let my client know."

ASSESSMENT TESTING

There are tons of tests you can use to determine how a candidate will perform. The Myers-Briggs Type Indicator, DiSC, predictive index, online, offline, internal psych testing—they all attempt to uncover people's strengths and weakness, inherent propensities, underlying personality traits and so on. Testing has a place in hiring, but it's not the end all and be all.

I recently interviewed someone for a sales position. Part of the assignment was to do assessment testing, so I had the candidate, Robert, take a DiSC test. Robert didn't describe himself as a leader, but rather as an influencer and part of his narrative after he took the assessment was that he liked to tell stories and engage people. When I interviewed him, I got the impression that Robert was indeed a great influencer, the kind of person who could take on a sales call.

People also tended to connect with him, but he's wasn't a details person, nor was he a closer. I needed a closer, so I passed on Robert. For that particular case, the results of the assessment were not surprising and confirmed what I already uncovered.

I have, however, interviewed people who have an incredible track record, but whose assessments test don't necessarily capture those achievements. When you go to test them, they usually don't score as high in the analytics portion of the exam, yet they are usually fantastic at their job. That's to say that assessment testing isn't fool-proof and should be used as one of many pieces in the hiring tool kit.

WHAT'S IN A REFERENCE?

References are never going to give you the full skinny on a candidate. Keep in mind that references are always handpicked to give a ringing endorsement. Instead of using references as a perfunctory part of the hiring process, use them as a method for onboarding a candidate. You can call them up to give you insight into how an employee might best transition to a new role, if you should check in on them or if you should be more hands-off. Some employees, when starting out, do really well with positive praise while others may not need as much external validation. Ask the reference: "What kind of coaching does the candidate need? Are there certain types of situations to avoid? Are they considerate to their fellow workers? Why did they leave? Do you miss them sometimes when you need help on a project?" You still owe it to yourself to glean some information from online social media profiles, but don't underestimate the power of a reference.

EAT, DRINK, AND FEEL THE FIT

The last part of the hiring process, even after checking in with references, is to see how a candidate behaves in public. How does it feel to go out for drinks with them? How do they treat the wait staff? Interacting with people outside of the office is another crucial indicator of cultural fit. Whether it's the holiday party at a bowling alley or a meeting the Four Seasons, if you know that someone can't get along with others in the relevant environment, then it's not a match. Going the extra mile to take a potential hire out for a coffee or a drink before making the final decisions could save you from disappointment down the line. There are, however, some good actors out there and I can't think of anyone who hasn't been fooled by an empty suit.

"Ok, would you two consider a job share?"

CHAPTER EIGHT:

THE EMPTY SUIT

A MASTER SUIT

Enough about hiring good candidates for now; what about avoiding those who bring nothing to the company? How do we keep from hiring an empty suit?

An empty suit is someone who makes themselves out to be much more able or important than they are—someone who is not particularly good at their job.

These masterminds of getting ahead without credentials can be found in small and large organizations throughout the world. We meet them at conferences, client meetings, interviews and even on vacations. They may be the best-dressed guy in the room, but they're Exhibit A of style over substance. Who are these posers who wear empty suits? Why do they always speak in platitudes? How do they get away with recycling others' suggestions and showing no original thought of their own? Maybe they're a relative of the CEO, or maybe they're the ones who ingratiate themselves by never saying "no" for fear of not getting the job, losing the client or impressing their staff.

Most of us know someone who has climbed up the corporate ladder into positions of authority that they don't deserve or aren't able to maintain. Many of these individuals are masters of performance, from the interview on down. "Oh yes, I sold over five million dollars last year." Then you find out, much too late, that the five million dollars was in the pipeline and closing the deal was another story. Many hiring managers have made this mistake and wound up saying, "Boy, he turned out to be an empty suit." Again, in the interview, let me stress language as a warning signal. Repeat questions by wording them differently. Press the candidate for detailed examples of their achievements and ask if you can call their client should an offer be extended.

THE EMPTY SUIT GUIDE

How do we identify and avoid the empty suit?

The generic empty suit can be broken down into three basic categories: high-level executive; rising MBA; and salesman.

Usually, the best place to go looking for empty suits is in large organizations since they have nowhere to hide in smaller, more entrepreneurial companies. Harvey Hornstein, a Columbia University Professor of Psychology and Education, and author of *Managerial Courage* has been studying the organizational environments that lead people to be more or less self-aware of their capabilities. He says, "When employees go in for self-scrutiny, they tend to speak up more, even against the prevailing wisdom, and may act more creatively." Empty suits tend not to speak up and don't like to go against the tide. Hornstein's research suggests that these pretenders tend to be "in organizations that favor hierarchy over participation, formality over warmth, and uniformity over pluralism."[15]

In a corporate environment where rules and procedures are valued over creativity and strategic thinking, the empty suit has ample opportunity to focus on political correctness without putting much effort into the work. If the standard corporate drill is to have a weekly meeting, they will show up to that meeting, devotedly, every Monday morning. They'll go through the motions of what's expected, but won't be concerned with generating new ideas or strategies—or with any other meeting outcome.

From time to time I've met an empty suit who came up through a corporate system that rotates people into a new position every 18 months. That was Phil's story. He was working as a VP in a large analytics company and he was in the middle of rotations, learning the ropes of each department. At each level of the company, people gravitated to Phil's persona because he sounded good. He talked the talk and walked the walk. Yet, he could never dive deep into any single task, being limited in the amount of time he could spend in each department. Eventually, rotations ended and Phil was placed in some permanent position. He hadn't received enough training during each rotation, nor had he gotten to know his teammates. As a result, he totally screwed up the few decisions he was compelled to make and in this company, screwing up wasn't tolerated. Phil knew he wasn't doing well, but he had nowhere to go and say, "I need help!" By the time fingers were pointing, he had flown the coop, and the remaining team had to clean up the mess. The lesson here is that sometimes, companies inadvertently create empty suits. Obviously

---

15 Hornstein, Harvey A. *Managerial Courage: Revitalizing Your Company without Sacrificing Your Job.* Wiley, 1986.

this is never intentional, but certain structures allow employees like Phil to work their way up and ultimately crash before they have the proper tools to cope.

"The typical empty suit, you see, is not an idiot," says David Campbell of the Center for Creative Leadership. "He may be bright and effective, but in a very predictable, very cubby-hole way. Call him 'Mr. Expedient.' As such, he can come in particularly handy at an organization still suffering the aftershocks of restructuring: Others have their heads down, desperately trying to avoid calling attention to themselves."[16] It's not unusual during restructuring that management wants to tie up loose ends such as additional cost-cutting and reducing staff. What the empty suit does best is brown-nosing the brass. He's a master performer and uses his charm to seduce. He goes out of his way to position himself with just the right person.

A master empty suit will have a succession of glamour jobs on their résumé. I once fell for this type of empty suit. She looked the part and talked a good game. But I should have looked more closely at her background; she didn't have long tenures at each position, and her career ended prematurely in the arena where she claimed to be highly networked, but when she joined the team, she didn't reach out to her database. It was a waste of time and money, not to mention leaving a bitter taste in our company.

RECOGNIZING THE EMPTY SUIT

The higher the position, the longer it takes to tell if someone is doing a good job. It's important to realize that just because someone is in a

---

16 Weinstein, Erika. "How to Avoid Hiring an Empty Suit." iMedia, October 24, 2014. http://www.imediaconnection.com/article/133392/how-to-avoid-hiring-an-empty-suit.

leadership position, it doesn't necessarily mean they should be. The problem many organizations suffer from is a recognition problem— they can't seem to recognize good leaders from bad ones. Brian Wong, CEO of the internet advertising company Kiip, says there are certain characteristics he looks for to avoid hiring an empty suit; "I want to understand if they are a good teacher. By nature are they patient, knowledgeable and giving?" Brian also explores people's "super power." Yes, you hear him right! He asks interviewees, "What's your super power?" Basically, what are you so great at that we can leverage and focus your energy on to minimize ramp-up time?

Anthony Reddish, Digital VP for the digital creative fashion agency MODCo Creative, relates a story of interviewing an executive in the digital design space. To get at the candidate's critical and creative thinking abilities, he asked her, "What was your goal when you created that website, and why did you create something in a certain way?" When she couldn't be specific in her answers, he realized that she was not the strategic thinker she purported to be. In fact, she was the junior person on the team.

The lesson Anthony learned here is that "honesty is key." Be authentic and do your homework, especially in digital arenas which change by the nano-second. Up your game, read the latest blogs and articles, stay current and constantly ask questions.

"Don't be the hamster in the wheel," advises Wong when referencing a staff member who'd "shoot off 10 words to communicate complex strategies with his team." He says, "that is pure laziness, and his team had no idea what's going on." Sometimes it pays to be simple and specific.

BEWARE THE EMPTY SUIT

We have all met, hired and worked with a "suit." But we've also probably seen that those who lack integrity tend not to endure the test of time. It doesn't matter how intelligent, affable, persuasive or savvy a person is, if they are prone to rationalizing ineffectual performance or unethical behavior based on current or future needs, they will eventually fall prey to their own undoing.

GOLDEN RULE: No one is perfect...

We are all subject to failure. Leaders who consistently fail are not leaders. They don't learn from their mistakes, but tend to blame others for their stumbles. Don't underestimate a long-term track record of success. Someone who has consistently experienced success in leadership roles has a much better chance of future triumphs than someone who has not.

*"No, I wasn't sleeping,
I'm always up at 4AM."*

CHAPTER NINE:

LOVE IN (AND OUT) OF THE OFFICE

LOVING YOUR JOB

There's lots to be said about being happy at work. Job satisfaction affects your well-being and it can also positively affect the people around you—your family, friends and colleagues. If you're like me, you want to work with others who love their jobs too, because employees who feel fulfilled are more fun to be around.

Engaged employees are more productive, efficient, and they're less likely to leave, which indicates a successful workplace for many leaders. According to Deloitte's 2014 Global Human Capital Trends research, 78 percent of business leaders rated retention and engagement as urgent or important.[17] Yet it's concerning that, while the majority of leaders say it's important to have satisfied employees, employee engagement is abysmally low on a national scale. In its

---

17 Deloitte Consulting LLP and Bersin by Deloitte. "Global Human Capital Trends 2014: Engaging the 21st-Century Workforce." *Deloitte University Press*, n.d. https://www2.deloitte.com/content/dam/Deloitte/ar/Documents/human-capital/arg_hc_global-human-capital-trends-2014_09062014%20(1).pdf.

third "State of the American Workplace" report published in 2017, Gallup found that employee engagement has increased slightly since 2012. Yet, the statistic still hovers at a relatively low number, reporting that only a third of American workers are engaged at work.[18] The same holds true even for those at the top. As Kevin Sheridan, author of *Building a Magnetic Culture*, points out, the greatest companies (those which scored in the top 10 percent on employee surveys) register only 38 percent of employees as "fully engaged."[19] Low employee engagement means the economy suffers from lost productivity costs. It means unattained riches and it means unhappy people. That is to say, if we don't meet the demand for holistic work environments that take employee well-being into consideration soon enough, the new generation of workers will lose out on achieving their full potential. How do we change this?

Many companies opt to offer corporate perks to their employees such as catered in-office lunches, game rooms, company off-sites or generous raises/ bonuses. While these perks may boost engagement in the short-term, they may not always produce the desired effect in the long-term. Daniel H. Pink, author of the 2009 bestseller *Drive*, describes these sorts of perks as "carrot-and-stick motivators."[20] According to Pink, they don't work in the long term, because they shift focus from the job itself to the reward. What we really want in our jobs, Pink argues, is a purpose that connects us to something larger.

---

18 Gallup Inc. "State of the American Workplace," 2017. https://news.gallup.com/reports/199961/7.aspx.
19 Sheridan, Kevin. *Building a Magnetic Culture: How to Attract and Retain Top Talent to Create an Engaged, Productive Workforce.* McGraw Hill Professional, 2011.
20 Pink, Daniel H. *Drive: The Surprising Truth About What Motivates Us.* Penguin, 2011.

It's no secret that people are prioritizing work that brings them a sense of purpose. In 2018, Deloitte titled its annual report "The Rise of the Social Enterprise," reflecting a corporate shift towards social responsibility. The 2018 report notes that organizations today are judged less on their financial performance and increasingly more on "the basis of their relationships with their workers, their customers, and their communities, as well as their impact on society at large–– transforming them from *business* enterprises into *social* enterprises."[21] Now more than ever, companies are expected to contribute to a healthy social ecosystem, which starts with treating their employees well. So, how do we give our employees purpose?

PURPOSE EQUALS ENGAGEMENT

Be sure your team understands the company's mission and vision. Purpose is the reason we get up in the morning and do our jobs. Without a sense of purpose, we would be navigating the high-seas without a compass. This is especially true for Millennials. According to a Pew Research Center report, 35% of American labor force participants are Millennials. That's the largest generation in the U.S. workforce today.[22] Studies show that these young professionals will work for a significantly lower salary if they believe in the job they are doing. Therefore, it is imperative that companies keep in mind their mission and communicate that purpose when hiring the new generation of workers, otherwise you can kiss your brightest employees goodbye!

---

21 Deloitte Insights. "2018 Global Human Capital Trends: The Rise of the Social Enterprise;" March 28, 2018. https://www2.deloitte.com/insights/us/en/focus/human-capital-trends.html.
22 Pew Research Center. "Millennials Are Largest Generation in the U.S. Labor Force." April 11, 2018. http://www.pewresearch.org/fact-tank/2018/04/11/millennials-largest-generation-us-labor-force/.

EMPLOYEE ENGAGEMENT

When we think about what measures we can take to make sure our employees love their jobs, the first thing that comes to mind is the elusive yet ubiquitous term: employee engagement. What does employee engagement really mean?

Gallup says engaged employees are those who are "highly involved in and enthusiastic about their work and workplace. They are psychological 'owners,' drive performance and innovation, and move the organization forward." I believe this concept of engagement is limiting. Our goal shouldn't be solely to increase business, but also to maintain happy and realized individuals. Why set our sights on mere output when we could be encouraging employees to bring their whole, authentic selves to work? It's up to corporate leaders to prioritize the happiness factor. Employee engagement needs to go from a yearly HR measure to a valued tenet of our businesses each day.

The best way to assess how your employees feel about their jobs is to ask them! Build relationships with your employees. Be aware of what is going on in your company. Ask employees for their opinions and advice. Give them ownership of their work and acknowledge them when they've done a great job. But don't go overboard; you also need to tell them what's expected every day.

Our objective when we communicate with our teams is to inspire passion. And as you can surmise by now, passion is an indispensable quality in business. Show me a switched-on leader and I will show you a successful leader.

FREEDOM IN THE GIG ECONOMY

Another emerging trend is the rise of the 1099 worker, aka the free-lancer. Its projected that by the year 2020, 50% of the workforce will be made up of freelancers.[23] These up-and-coming professionals are building their careers by working for themselves, relying largely on freelance-based work rather than on full-time, salaried positions. Why are people happy about this? Because it means freedom and flexibility! Since Millennials are not necessarily driven by money like their predecessors, and are more concerned about the environment, social change and adaptability, this new generation is taking advantage of the gig economy and tailoring it to their own interests and needs. In its seventh annual Millennial Survey, Deloitte researchers (who included Generation Z in its report for the first time) found that young workers are showing less loyalty to and confidence in business. Based on recent political events and eroding confidence in institutions, in 2018 less than half of Millennials reported that they feel business behave ethically and that business leaders are committed to helping improve society. Since these generations "place a premium on factors like tolerance and inclusivity," employers perceived to have diverse workforces and senior management teams are more likely to retain employees from these younger generations. Another face of this eroding confidence is that more people enjoy being employed by themselves, viewing freelance work and work in the gig economy as viable alternative or adjunct to their jobs.[24]

23 Rashid, Brian. "The Rise Of The Freelancer Economy." *Forbes*, January 26, 2016. https://www.forbes.com/sites/brianrashid/2016/01/26/the-rise-of-the-freelancer-economy/
24 Deloitte. "Millennial Survey 2018 | Deloitte | Social Impact, Innovation," May 15, 2018. https://www2.deloitte.com/global/en/pages/about-deloitte/articles/millennialsurvey.html.

This attitude is permeating many industries, not just in startups like Uber or Lyft. The *Wall Street Journal* reported in 2017 that, "at large firms, 20% to 50% of the total workforce often is outsourced."[25] While it can be difficult to predict how this will affect the workforce, the emergence of the 1099 worker has potential to be beneficial to both parties: the freelancer and the organizations hiring them. Not only does working on a freelance basis give these workers the flexibility to create their own schedules, allowing them to widen the depth and breadth of their work, but it also keeps them engaged. This generation grew up with video games, snapchat and social media providing them with instant stimuli at any moment. With more part-time and temporary work available, these young professionals don't have to be graphic designers for just one company, they can be graphic designers for five companies and even set their calendars and pick the projects they want to work on. Temporary work is becoming attractive and many are choosing to take it on as a permanent path. With the freedom to explore multiple paths at once, Millennials have great opportunity for finding out what they're good at and how they can apply their skills to different jobs.

Of course we also live in an era of transparency, so the rise of the gig economy is a double-edged sword for both the employee and the employer. As a freelancer, if you don't show up for a job or turn something in late, it will come back to bite you in the ass! It's likely you won't be referred to other companies or organizations. Conversely, if you're an employer and you don't pay your 1099 employee, people will chase after you on social media, and that will also come back to bite you in the ass! Playing fair in the sandbox is more important now than any other time in the history of working.

25 Weber, Lauren. "The End of Employees." *The Wall Street Journal*, February 2, 2017.

Many have criticized the Millennial generation as being selfish, seeking instant gratification and whining about anything they deem an injustice. But if you really dissect this generation and look at the events leading up to their launch into the workforce, you see a pattern of overlapping trends. Millennials were raised in the shadow of the 9/11 attacks, with helicopter parents afraid of their kids walking out of the door. Combine that with the fact that everything is available to them through the Internet; you can go shopping from your bed, you can learn from downloadable online classes and chat with friends over messaging apps. Our culture of convenience had led many to label Millennials as lazy, but I would argue that this generation is simply pushing us to adapt to the times. Management from X and Y generations, who are much more serious, have to recognize as leaders that employees are looking for personal enjoyment and the pursuit of happiness. Baby boomers worked to pay the rent. Millennials work to facilitate their passions and the money is secondary. If we want to motivate workers in this generation, we have to find inspiration.

INSPIRE ME

Amongst all these changes toward social responsibility and the emerging gig economy, there is one consistent factor among successful people and organizations—inspiration. Many of us would agree that inspiration is the key to motivation. It urges us to try new things and drives us to put forward our best effort, both in the workplace and in our relationships. Without inspiration, our lives would be dull and mundane.

A while ago, I attended a Luxury Marketing Council event centered around "Galvanizing Corporate Culture: Inspiring People to Perform."

Steve Cody, Co-founder and Managing partner of Peppercomm, a digital communications agency, said it best: "Management sets the stage and often the person in the corner office sets the tone." Inspiring your team to bring your brand's vision and mission to life is not an easy task. The speed of business today keeps CEOs on their toes, and often they leave inspiration out of the corporate equation. In order for your company to thrive, your employees need to be jazzed.

At the same time, no one likes a control freak. Leave room for diversity of thought and style so your employees feel they are part of the organization. One company I feel does a great job at nailing this balance is Rolex.

ROLEX--UNDERSTATED PERFECTION

Considered one of the most reputable brands in the world, charity and giving are an intrinsic part of the Rolex culture. The brand evolved, as did its product, in a constant pursuit of perfection. Watches are made from the finest materials and designed by the industry's best. The Swiss watchmaker has become a symbol of elegance, prestige and the highest performance. To preserve this long-standing tradition and reputation, Rolex only hires star performers and continues to make giving part of its core culture.

I'm always impressed with anyone I meet associated with Rolex. Their employees reflect the ethics of the brand. They are not snooty or show-offy, as one might expect, but are rather quite humble and content. They know they are the best; they believe in their product and organization, and they don't need to flaunt it for the rest of the world to see. Their work ethic and demeanor must uphold the tradition of excellence that the Rolex name represents. I believe the brand stands as a good example of infusing its mission and ethics into company culture and thus inspiring its employees to act with sophistication.

ZAPPOS--FEEL THE LOVE

Zappos, the online shoe retailer, is well-known for its fantastic company culture. Zappos founder and CEO Tony Hsieh is very involved in his company's culture and is focuses on maintaining a set of ten core values, optimizing how employees fit in culturally. To maximize the well-being of his employees' and company's health, Zappos hires based on cultural fit, which accounts for 50% of the weight in a hiring decision. Once employees are onboarded, they are offered $3,000 to leave within the first two weeks if they don't feel it's the right job for them. On top of this, Hsieh has dedicated a team to train employees in each core value of the company, which range from "create fun and a little weirdness" to "do more with less," so that everyone is on the same page and fueled by the same mission.[26] Hsieh's involvement at every stage of cultural development is then reflected in his customer service and translated to his customers. In an interview with *Marketplace*, Hsieh expanded on why company culture is so important to him: "For us our number one priority as a company is company culture, and our whole belief is that if we get the culture right then most of the other stuff like delivering great customer service or building a long-term enduring brand will just happen naturally on its own."[27] When cultural fit takes precedence over hiring for specific skills, the result is happy employees who love coming into work every day and being part of the team.

26 Heathfield, Susan M. "Find Out How Zappos Reinforces Its Company Culture." *The Balance Careers* (blog), September 21, 2018. https://www.thebalancecareers.com/zappos-company-culture-1918813.
27 Ryssdal, Kai. "Zappos CEO Tony Hsieh." *Marketplace*, August 19, 2010. http://www.marketplace.org/2010/08/19/business/corner-office/zappos-ceo-tony-hsieh-full-interview-transcript.

LOVE CONQUERS ALL

The importance of inspiring your team can't be overstated. Be sure to sprinkle some of that unicorn dust on your clients as well. If your clients don't feel your passion, then why would they do business with you or your company? Passion often builds the heart and the heart builds trust.

When you love your job, you bring your entire repertoire of skills to the table. When you place your heart into your work, your colleagues feel it and are inspired to follow suit. So start loving your job because the rewards are immeasurable. And if you don't love what you do, start looking for something else that you'll love. Life is short!

CHAPTER TEN:

HIRING IN THE AGE OF TRANSPARENCY

Social media, the "age of transparency," makes it difficult to sift through fact and fiction. How do you determine actual events vs. opinion? News vs. fake news? Do you believe everything on the Internet? If something is repeated over time, does it become a fact or reputation?

Now more than ever, people are getting their news from social media, which also happens to be where your employees, your peers, and your competition are all talking. In this day and age, we have to be aware of how social media is impacting business and hiring practices. How you behave today, either as an employee or as a business executive, will affect you tomorrow. Human resources departments and recruiters will have to alter their practices, particularly on social media, in order to adapt to the transparent age. Furthermore, as we begin to renegotiate what's appropriate in the workplace, organizations of all ranks are going to have to take a hard look at company practices to keep up with the social changes, or face the consequences. Let's take a look at a few major trends driving this new age: social media and the #MeToo movement.

SOCIAL MEDIA

Think about how many times you got a job by simply sending in a résumé. I imagine the numbers are pretty low or close to none. Networking and connections have always facilitated the flow of hiring and now, social media is enhancing this phenomenon. With platforms like Facebook, Twitter and LinkedIn, recruiters have a vast amount of information about a candidate right at their fingertips. Yet, even with all this new information, the process can sometimes be overwhelming, especially when it comes to choosing a passionate candidate with the right cultural fit. Recruiters can now source through social media and find "passive candidates," or those who aren't actively looking for a new job.[28] For instance, recruiters can learn a lot about a person's personality from blog posts or newsfeed updates in addition to résumé skills from platforms like LinkedIn. How much of a factor should someone's social media persona play into our hiring decisions? How will that affect bias in hiring when everything is out in the open?

Social media contributes to the heightened flow of information, and with it, a somewhat volatile environment of public shaming, affecting employees large and small. Take Talia Jane, a customer service rep who was fired for publishing an open letter to her CEO. In February 2016 Talia, who was working for Yelp's Eat24 branch, published a letter addressed to CEO Jeremy Stoppelman on *Medium,* claiming that her low pay living in the high-cost Bay Area was causing her to struggle paying for rent and groceries.[29] She wrote, "So here I am,

28 See: Fennessey, Geri. "Hiring in the Age of Transparency" *Talent Management,* March 11, 2015. https://talentmgt.com/2015/03/11/hiring-in-the-age-of-transparency__trashed/.
29 Chew, Jonathan. "Yelp Fired an Employee After She Wrote a Post About Her Lousy Pay." *Fortune Magazine,* February 22, 2016. http://fortune.com/2016/02/22/yelp-employee-ceo/.

25-years old, balancing all sorts of debt and trying to pave a life for myself that doesn't involve crying in the bathtub every week. Every single one of my coworkers is struggling. They're taking side jobs, they're living at home. One of them started a GoFundMe because she couldn't pay her rent." Talia published the letter on a Friday afternoon. Although the CEO responded on Twitter, saying that he had read the post and "want[s] to acknowledge her point that the cost of living in SF is far too high. I have been focused on this issue, backing anti-NIMBY group SFBARF and speaking out frequently about the need to lower cost of housing," she was fired the following Monday. We don't know what their exact thinking was which led to their actions. We can draw our own conclusions, that social media should not be used as a public airing of personal and corporate issues. Perhaps the course of action could have been an internal memo versus a public tongue lashing. We also might come to the conclusion that this is not a forgiving culture and doesn't support their employees outside of the workplace.

There are numerous examples of using social media as a communication tool and having it backfire. Looking at the now infamous example of Justine Sacco, the former senior director of corporate communications at IAC, we see a common thread. Justine was fired for a Tweet she sent while boarding a plane to South Africa that many interpreted as racist. "Going to Africa. Hope I don't get AIDS. Just kidding. I'm white!" [30] She was justly fired immediately. Social media is a communication tool that creates transparency––be careful, it can come back to bite you.

30 Ronson, Jon. "How One Stupid Tweet Blew Up Justine Sacco's Life." *The New York Times Magazine*, February 12, 2015. https://www.nytimes.com/2015/02/15/magazine/how-one-stupid-tweet-ruined-justine-saccos-life.html.

We're just beginning to understand how social media transforms the work environment and it's up to leaders to anticipate methods for moderating our online presence. In an essay for *MIT Sloan Management Review*, authors Robert D. Austin and David M. Upton lay out the myriad of ways that, what they call "super-transparency," can impact business even beyond social media posting.[31] They note the instant sharing of provocative images, videos and stories, which commonly bypass the traditional vetting of news and media outlets, has incited a wave of changes that business are only beginning to understand. For instance in many parts of the world, most people have a smartphone as their disposal most of the time. With that number increasing exponentially, so too does the amount of information being shared. The authors argue that this flow of data interacts with other networks in such a tightly, interconnected way, to produce "amplification" which, "causes information to feed back upon itself. People are drawn in not only by the original message but also by *reactions* to it (and reactions to *reactions*)."

THE #METOO MOVEMENT

There is also a positive side of enhanced transparency. At the same time social media is transforming the hiring landscape, the emergence of the #MeToo movement is impacting how companies operate internally. The wave of women's stories about sexual assault and harassment in the workplace going public, revealing the prevalence of such instances in a range of industries, is capitalizing on the era of enhanced transparency to bring down people who misbehave. With a push from activists and leaders, many people are facing consequences for their actions who may not have otherwise been exposed.

---

31 Austin, Robert D., and David M. Upton. "Leading in the Age of Super-Transparency." *MIT Sloan Management Review* 57, no. 2 (Winter 2016). https:// shop.sloanreview.mit.edu/store/leading-in-the-age-of-super-transparency

Before #MeToo took center stage, people largely kept bad behavior in the workplace (e.g., harassment, ageism, racism, sexism) to themselves. We were either embarrassed or indifferent to the comments, afraid of the repercussions. Social Media has given employees a voice, and now we're going to have to look inside ourselves, our companies and our communications to determine what's appropriate and inappropriate. Office rules and etiquette are changing with the speed of our media and its confusing for people to figure out how to behave. Companies will have to redefine their guidelines in order to adapt to changing social moralities.

I often hear from young people, if you're allowed to say things like, "you look beautiful today" or "that's a nice outfit." These concerns echo the same questions many of us are asking about our bosses, like if it's appropriate for a superior to say "you fucked up!" The anxiety following #MeToo has stirred up the way we relate to each other in the workplace, forcing us to reevaluate the old standards of conduct.

Many people wonder, are we going to sacrifice honesty for appropriateness and political correctness? It's one thing to talk about someone personally and in my opinion, that doesn't belong in the workplace. I do, however, believe that we need to maintain the freedom to talk about work output and if goals are being met. Don't confuse management with political correctness. You need to get the job done, and you need to communicate what's going well and what's going wrong. People are rightfully confused at where to draw the line, and leaders are going to have to step up and lay it out for their employees, no matter how difficult the process may be.

Leaders should be in direct communication with their employees about what's appropriate, besides it being in the guidelines. No CEO should be above walking through the lunch room and having an open and honest conversation with all employees, regardless of their title. There's no excuse anymore. Now that everything is transparent, we're also going to have to break down some of the traditional hierarchical barriers.

FINAL THOUGHTS

Hiring is the most important skill to growing your business. It's not about the perfect employee or job, because there is no such thing as perfect. Instead look for the ideal or find your passion. Does your company culture reflect your feelings and vision? Do you have the "right" people on the proverbial bus? Take your time, think about goals and expectations. Are you realistic?

Successful people, whether they are leaders or employees, are passionate people. Think of your ideal vision as a road map, with passion as the race car and desire, the finish line. It's the passion we bring to our relationships that creates the willingness to practice, refine skills and ultimately achieve goals. Desire makes us strive for the next level. We need to delve into the passion before we hire or take a position. Ask yourself the question: "What is my passion?" "What gets me out of bed in the morning?"

If you ask people what's their true passion, most simply don't know or are unable to articulate it in an interview. Perhaps that's why job satisfaction is such a rare commodity in the workplace. If you really love what you do, you'll be successful... eventually!

GOLDEN RULES:

- Experimenting is the key to innovation

- When you are actively listening, it's really hard to f*ck up

- I'm never lost, I simply find new places

- Culture is not just having the core values of your company painted on the wall

- In hiring, there is no room for unrequited love

- Before you look outside for talent, look inside for the fire.

- There might be no "I" in "team," but there is a "me."

- Don't discuss the size of the ring until you fall in love

- Hiring should start with your leaders

- No one is perfect, we are all subject to failure

- Hire for change

- Talk the same language

- Listen to the new generation, there is wisdom to be found

WORKS CITED

Athlete Won't Let Dwarfism Stop Ironman Dream: John Young Is Hoping to Become the First Person with Dwarfism to Complete an Ironman Triathlon. CNN, n.d. https://www.cnn.com/videos/health/2016/11/18/fit-nation-ironman-john-young-dwarfism.cnn/video/playlists/fit-nation/.

Austin, Robert D., and David M. Upton. "Leading in the Age of Super-Transparency." *MIT Sloan Management Review 57,* no. 2 (Winter 2016). https://shop.sloanreview.mit.edu/store/leading-in-the-age-of-super-transparency.

Branson, Richard. "How I Hire: Focus On Personality." *LinkedIn* (blog), September 23, 2013. https://www.linkedin.com/pulse/20130923230007-204068115-how-i-hire-focus-on-personality/.

Brown, Tim. "How I Hire: 5 Tips for Landing a Job at IDEO." *LinkedIn* (blog), September 24, 2013. https://www.linkedin.com/pulse/20130924105210-10842349-how-i-hire-5-tips-for-landing-a-job-at-ideo/.

Carton, Andrew M. "'I'm Not Mopping the Floors, I'm Putting a Man on the Moon': How NASA Leaders Enhanced the Meaningfulness of Work by Changing the Meaning of Work." *Administrative Science Quarterly* 63, no. 2 (June 1, 2018): 323–69. https://doi.org/10.1177/0001839217713748.

Chew, Jonathan. "Yelp Fired an Employee After She Wrote a Post About Her Lousy Pay." *Fortune Magazine*, February 22, 2016. http://fortune.com/2016/02/22/yelp-employee-ceo/.

Deloitte. "Millennial Survey 2018 | Deloitte | Social Impact, Innovation," May 15, 2018. https://www2.deloitte.com/global/en/pages/about-deloitte/articles/millennialsurvey.html.

Deloitte Consulting LLP and Bersin by Deloitte. "Global Human Capital Trends 2014: Engaging the 21st-Century Workforce." Deloitte University Press, n.d. https://www2.deloitte.com/content/dam/Deloitte/ar/Documents/human-capital/arg_hc_global-human-capital-trends-2014_09062014%20(1).pdf.

Deloitte Insights. "2018 Global Human Capital Trends: The Rise of the Social Enterprise:," March 28, 2018. https://www2.deloitte.com/insights/us/en/focus/human-capital-trends.html.

Fennessey, Geri. "Hiring in the Age of Transparency – Talent Management." *Talent Management*, March

11, 2015. https://talentmgt.com/2015/03/11/
hiring-in-the-age-of-transparency__trashed/.

Gallup Inc. "State of the American Workplace," 2017. https://news.
gallup.com/reports/199961/7.aspx.

———. "State of the American Workplace: Employee Engagement
Insights for U.S. Business Leaders," 2013. http://www.gallup.com/
strategicconsulting/163007/state-american-workplace.aspx).
Google Scholar.

Glassdoor. "Blue Chip Marketing Worldwide Reviews." Glassdoor.
Accessed December 5, 2018. https://www.glassdoor.com/Reviews/
Blue-Chip-Marketing-Worldwide-Reviews-E403219.htm.

———. "Glassdoor's 2018 Best Places to Work: Employee Choice
Awards." Accessed November 14, 2018. https://www.glassdoor.com/
Award/Best-Places-to-Work-LST_KQ0,19.htm.

Heathfield, Susan M. "Find Out How Zappos Reinforces
Its Company Culture." *The Balance Careers* (blog),
September 21, 2018. https://www.thebalancecareers.com/
zappos-company-culture-1918813.

Hornstein, Harvey A. *Managerial Courage: Revitalizing Your
Company without Sacrificing Your Job*. Wiley, 1986.

Kelley, David. *How to Build Your Creative
Confidence*. TED, 2012. https://www.ted.com/talks/
david_kelley_how_to_build_your_creative_confidence.

Kelley, David, and Tom Kelley. "Reclaim Your Creative Confidence." *Harvard Business Review* 90, no. 12 (December 2012): 115–18.

Larssen, Adrian Granzella. "Mark Zuckerberg's #1 Hiring Rule (and What You Can Learn From It)." *The Muse,* March 13, 2015. https://www.themuse.com/advice/ mark-zuckerbergs-1-hiring-rule-and-what-you-can-learn-from-it.

Loretta Graziano Breuning. *Habits of a Happy Brain: Retrain Your Brain to Boost Your Serotonin, Dopamine, Oxytocin, & Endorphin Levels.* F + W Media, 2015. https://www.amazon.com/ Habits-Happy-Brain-Serotonin-Endorphin/dp/1440590508.

McCracken, Harry. "How Facebook Keeps Scaling Its Culture." *Fast Company,* November 24, 2015. https://www.fastcompany. com/3053776/how-facebook-keeps-scaling-its-culture.

Penttila, Chris. "Managing the 'Lone Wolf.'" *Entrepreneur,* April 1, 2005. https://www.entrepreneur.com/article/76968.

Pew Research Center. "Millennials Are Largest Generation in the U.S. Labor Force." Accessed November 16, 2018. http://www.pewresearch.org/fact-tank/2018/04/11/ millennials-largest-generation-us-labor-force/.

Pink, Daniel H. *Drive: The Surprising Truth About What Motivates Us.* Penguin, 2011.

Rashid, Brian. "The Rise Of The Freelancer Economy." *Forbes,* January 26, 2016. https://www.forbes.com/sites/ brianrashid/2016/01/26/the-rise-of-the-freelancer-economy/

Ronson, Jon. "How One Stupid Tweet Blew Up Justine Sacco's Life." *The New York Times Magazine*, February 12, 2015. https://www.nytimes.com/2015/02/15/magazine/how-one-stupid-tweet-ruined-justine-saccos-life.html.

Ryssdal, Kai. "Zappos CEO Tony Hsieh." *Marketplace*, August 19, 2010. http://www.marketplace.org/2010/08/19/business/corner-office/zappos-ceo-tony-hsieh-full-interview-transcript.

Sheridan, Kevin. *Building a Magnetic Culture: How to Attract and Retain Top Talent to Create an Engaged, Productive Workforce.* McGraw Hill Professional, 2011.

Sinek, Simon. *Leaders Eat Last: Why Some Teams Pull Together and Others Don't*. Penguin, 2014.

The Staff Of Entrepreneur Media Inc. *Entrepreneur Voices on Company Culture*. Edited by Derek Lewis. Entrepreneur Media Incorporated/Entrepreneur Press, 2018.

Weber, Lauren. "The End of Employees." *The Wall Street Journal*, February 2, 207AD.

Weinstein, Erika. "How to Avoid Hiring an Empty Suit." iMedia, October 24, 2014. http://www.imediaconnection.com/article/133392/how-to-avoid-hiring-an-empty-suit.

White, Gillian B. "Millennials Are Searching for a Different Kind of Career." *CityLab*. Accessed November 16, 2018. http://www.citylab.com/work/2015/06/millennials-are-in-search-of-a-different-kind-of-career/395717/.